Barista Creations: 101 Recipes and Expert Tips

The French Toastery

Copyright © 2023 The French Toastery
All rights reserved.
:

Contents

INTRODUCTION 7
1. Espresso 9
2. Cappuccino 10
3. Latte 11
4. Mocha 12
5. Americano 13
6. Flat White 14
7. Macchiato 16
8. Affogato 17
9. Irish Coffee 17
10. Frappuccino 18
11. Iced Coffee 19
12. Turkish Coffee 20
13. Vietnamese Coffee 21
14. Cortado 22
15. Breve 23
16. Ristretto 24
17. Doppio 25
18. Lungo 26
19. Espresso Martini 28
20. Pumpkin Spice Latte 29
21. Hazelnut Latte 30
22. Vanilla Latte 30
23. Caramel Macchiato 31
24. White Chocolate Mocha 32
25. Peppermint Mocha 33
26. Coconut Mocha 34
27. Almond Milk Latte 35

28. Soy Milk Latte 36

29. Oat Milk Latte 37

30. Cold Brew 38

31. Nitro Cold Brew 39

32. Iced Caramel Macchiato 39

33. Iced Vanilla Latte 41

34. Iced Matcha Latte 42

35. Iced Chai Latte 43

36. Iced Coconut Mocha 44

37. Iced Hazelnut Latte 45

38. Iced Almond Milk Latte 46

39. Iced Soy Milk Latte 47

40. Iced Oat Milk Latte 48

41. Espresso Con Panna 49

42. Vienna Coffee 50

43. Caramel Cappuccino 51

44. White Mocha Latte... 53

45. Gingerbread Latte 53

46. Maple Pecan Latte 55

47. Cardamom Spiced Latte 56

48. Lavender Honey Latte 57

49. Raspberry Mocha.. 58

50. Nutella Latte 59

51. Cinnamon Dolce Latte 60

52. Salted Caramel Latte 61

53. Caramel Brulee Latte 62

54. Tiramisu Latte 63

55. Coconut Caramel Latte 64

56. Pistachio Mocha 65

57. Chocolate Mint Latte 66
58. Caramelized Banana Latte 67
59. Matcha Green Tea Latte 69
60. Golden Milk Latte 69
61. Irish Cream Latte 71
62. Raspberry White Mocha 72
63. Pumpkin Caramel Latte 73
64. Hazelnut White Mocha 73
65. Almond Joy Latte 74
66. Snickerdoodle Latte 75
67. Maple Cinnamon Latte 77
68. Pistachio White Mocha 78
69. Nutella Mocha 79
70. Spiced Apple Latte 80
71. Rosemary Honey Latte 82
72. S'mores Latte 83
73. Cinnamon Roll Latte 84
74. Peanut Butter Cup Latte 85
75. Strawberry Cheesecake Latte 86
76. Brown Sugar Caramel Latte 87
77. Cookies and Cream Latte 88
78. Mocha Cookie Crumble 88
79. Chocolate Coconut Latte 90
80. Cherry Almond Latte 91
81. Mint Chocolate Latte 92
82. Caramel Apple Latte 93
83. Blueberry Muffin Latte 94
84. Gingerbread White Mocha 95
85. Maple Bacon Latte 97

86. Chocolate Peanut Butter Latte 98
87. Spiced Pumpkin Chai Latte 98
88. Eggnog Latte 99
89. Cinnamon Hot Chocolate 100
90. White Hot Chocolate 101
91. Raspberry Hot Chocolate 103
92. Peppermint Hot Chocolate 104
93. Nutella Hot Chocolate 105
94. Salted Caramel Hot Chocolate 106
95. Caramel Apple Hot Chocolate 107
96. Mocha Hot Chocolate 108
97. Pumpkin Spice Hot Chocolate 109
98. Spiced Chai Hot Chocolate 110
99. Almond Joy Hot Chocolate 112
100. Cookies and Cream Hot Chocolate 113
101. S'mores Hot Chocolate 113
CONCLUSION 116

INTRODUCTION

Welcome to the world of Barista´s Coffee Creations! Coffee is one of the most popular and beloved morning rituals around the world, and this cookbook has been specifically designed to bring the unique flavor and art of coffee-making right to your kitchen. In this book, you will find 101 delicious recipes and pro tips that will help you brew perfect coffee drinks. Whether you are a novice or a connoisseur, you are sure to find something here that will help you produce amazing coffee.

Coffee has been around for centuries, and throughout the years it has been a part of many cultures and societies. Coffee beverages are as varied and diverse as the countries that produce them and this cookbook captures the flavors and characteristics of both traditional and modern coffee blends. It provides a variety of recipes made with diverse ingredients and comprehensive instructions to ensure great results every time.

The recipes in this cookbook range from traditional espresso-based drinks like Cappuccino and Lungo, to creative and flavorful mocha beverages. There are also recipes for hot chocolate and different flavors of ice coffee drinks. Each recipe provides detailed instructions and a list of ingredients, ensuring that you can produce the perfect coffee every time.

In addition to recipes, Barista´s Coffee Creations includes an array of expert tips, such as how to choose grind size, how to make the perfect espresso, and which accessories are necessary for creating a professional brew. Every recipe also features the best brewing recipes and techniques, as well as recommended serving suggestions.

Barista´s Coffee Creations is the perfect choice for those who are looking for an easy-to-follow, comprehensive guide to making delicious coffee and espresso-based drinks. Whether you are looking to create a classic, well-crafted cappuccino or a modern-twist on a mocha, this cookbook will provide you with the tools you need to ensure success each and every time. So, pour yourself a cup of coffee and get ready to explore the intriguing world of Barista´s Coffee Creations.

1. Espresso

Espresso is a strong and aromatic coffee beverage that originated in Italy. It is made by forcing hot water through finely ground coffee beans, resulting in a concentrated and flavorful drink. Espresso is the base for many popular coffee drinks such as cappuccinos and lattes. With its rich and bold flavor, it is the perfect pick-me-up for coffee lovers.
Serving: 1 cup
Preparation time: 5 minutes
Ready time: 5 minutes

Ingredients:
- 1 tablespoon finely ground espresso coffee beans
- 1 cup hot water

Instructions:
1. Start by grinding your coffee beans to a fine consistency. It is important to use freshly ground beans for the best flavor.
2. Measure out 1 tablespoon of the finely ground coffee and place it in the portafilter of your espresso machine.
3. Tamp down the coffee grounds firmly using a tamper to ensure even extraction.
4. Attach the portafilter to your espresso machine and place a cup underneath the spout.
5. Turn on the machine and let the hot water run through the coffee grounds. The water should be heated to around 195°F to 205°F (90°C to 96°C) for optimal extraction.
6. The espresso should start pouring into the cup in a steady stream. It should take around 25 to 30 seconds to extract 1 ounce (30ml) of espresso.
7. Once you have the desired amount of espresso, turn off the machine and remove the cup.
8. Give the espresso a quick stir to mix the crema, which is the golden foam on top, with the rest of the liquid.
9. Your espresso is now ready to be enjoyed as is or used as a base for other coffee drinks.

Nutrition information per Serving: - Calories: 2

- Fat: 0g
- Carbohydrates: 0g
- Protein: 0g
- Fiber: 0g
- Sugar: 0g
- Sodium: 0mg
- Caffeine: 63mg

Note: The nutrition information may vary depending on the brand of coffee beans used and the size of the serving.

2. Cappuccino

Cappuccino is a classic Italian coffee beverage that is loved by coffee enthusiasts all over the world. This creamy and frothy drink is the perfect way to start your day or enjoy a cozy afternoon break. Made with a combination of espresso, steamed milk, and a layer of velvety foam, cappuccino is a delightful treat that can be enjoyed at any time of the day.

Serving: 1 cup
Preparation time: 5 minutes
Ready time: 10 minutes

Ingredients:
- 1 shot of espresso
- 1 cup of milk
- 1 tablespoon of sugar (optional)
- Cocoa powder or cinnamon for garnish (optional)

Instructions:
1. Start by brewing a shot of espresso using an espresso machine or a stovetop espresso maker. Set it aside.
2. In a small saucepan, heat the milk over medium heat until it starts to steam. Be careful not to let it boil.
3. Once the milk is steaming, remove it from the heat and froth it using a milk frother or a whisk. If using a milk frother, follow the manufacturer's instructions.
4. Pour the espresso shot into a cup and add the desired amount of sugar, if using. Stir well to dissolve the sugar.

5. Slowly pour the frothed milk over the espresso, holding back the foam with a spoon to create a layered effect.
6. Spoon the remaining foam on top of the milk.
7. If desired, sprinkle some cocoa powder or cinnamon on top for garnish.
8. Serve the cappuccino immediately and enjoy!

Nutrition information:
- Calories: 120
- Fat: 4g
- Carbohydrates: 12g
- Protein: 8g
- Sugar: 10g
- Sodium: 100mg

3. Latte

Latte is a popular coffee-based beverage that originated in Italy. It is made by combining espresso with steamed milk, resulting in a creamy and delicious drink. Whether you enjoy it in the morning as a pick-me-up or as an afternoon treat, a latte is sure to satisfy your coffee cravings.
Serving: 1 Serving: Preparation time: 5 minutes
Ready time: 5 minutes

Ingredients:
- 1 shot of espresso
- 1 cup of milk
- 1 tablespoon of sugar (optional)
- Cocoa powder or cinnamon for garnish (optional)

Instructions:
1. Brew a shot of espresso using an espresso machine or a stovetop espresso maker.
2. In a small saucepan, heat the milk over medium heat until it starts to steam. Be careful not to let it boil.
3. If desired, add sugar to the milk and stir until dissolved.
4. Froth the milk using a milk frother or by vigorously whisking it until it becomes creamy and frothy.

5. Pour the espresso shot into a mug.
6. Slowly pour the frothed milk over the espresso, holding back the foam with a spoon to create a layered effect.
7. If desired, sprinkle cocoa powder or cinnamon on top for added flavor and decoration.
8. Serve immediately and enjoy your homemade latte!

Nutrition information per Serving: - Calories: 120
- Fat: 4g
- Carbohydrates: 12g
- Protein: 8g
- Sugar: 10g
- Sodium: 100mg
- Calcium: 250mg

Note: The nutrition information may vary depending on the type of milk and sugar used.

4. Mocha

Mocha is a delightful and indulgent beverage that combines the rich flavors of coffee and chocolate. This creamy and aromatic drink is perfect for those who love the combination of these two beloved flavors. Whether you enjoy it as a morning pick-me-up or as an after-dinner treat, Mocha is sure to satisfy your cravings for something sweet and caffeinated.

Serving: 1 Serving: Preparation time: 5 minutes
Ready time: 10 minutes

Ingredients:
- 1 cup of freshly brewed strong coffee
- 1 cup of milk
- 2 tablespoons of unsweetened cocoa powder
- 2 tablespoons of granulated sugar
- 1/4 teaspoon of vanilla extract
- Whipped cream (optional)
- Chocolate shavings (optional)

Instructions:

1. In a small saucepan, heat the milk over medium heat until it starts to steam. Do not let it boil.
2. In a separate bowl, whisk together the cocoa powder and sugar until well combined.
3. Slowly pour the hot milk into the cocoa powder mixture, whisking constantly to dissolve any lumps.
4. Add the vanilla extract to the mixture and stir well.
5. Pour the freshly brewed coffee into the cocoa mixture and stir until everything is well combined.
6. Taste the Mocha and adjust the sweetness according to your preference by adding more sugar if desired.
7. Pour the Mocha into a mug and top it with whipped cream and chocolate shavings if desired.
8. Serve the Mocha hot and enjoy!

Nutrition information:
- Calories: 150
- Fat: 4g
- Carbohydrates: 25g
- Protein: 6g
- Sugar: 18g
- Fiber: 3g
- Sodium: 80mg

5. Americano

Americano is a classic American coffee beverage that is loved by coffee enthusiasts all around the world. It is a simple yet delicious drink that combines the boldness of espresso with the smoothness of hot water. Whether you enjoy it in the morning to kickstart your day or as an afternoon pick-me-up, the Americano is sure to satisfy your coffee cravings.
Serving: 1 cup
Preparation time: 5 minutes
Ready time: 5 minutes

Ingredients:
- 1 shot of espresso

- Hot water
- Sugar or sweetener (optional)
- Milk or cream (optional)

Instructions:
1. Start by brewing a shot of espresso using an espresso machine or a stovetop espresso maker. If you don't have an espresso machine, you can use a strong brewed coffee instead.
2. Once the espresso is ready, pour it into a cup.
3. Fill the cup with hot water, leaving some space at the top for any additional Ingredients you may want to add.
4. If desired, add sugar or sweetener to taste. Stir well to dissolve.
5. If you prefer a creamy Americano, add a splash of milk or cream. Stir gently to combine.
6. Your Americano is now ready to be enjoyed! Serve it hot and savor the rich flavors.

Nutrition information:
- Calories: 5
- Fat: 0g
- Carbohydrates: 1g
- Protein: 0g
- Sugar: 0g
- Sodium: 5mg
- Caffeine: 63mg

Note: The nutrition information may vary depending on the specific brands and quantities of Ingredients used.

6. Flat White

Flat White is a popular coffee beverage that originated in Australia and New Zealand. It is made by pouring microfoam (steamed milk with small, fine bubbles) over a shot of espresso. The result is a smooth and velvety coffee with a rich flavor. This recipe will guide you on how to make a delicious Flat White at home.

Serving: 1 cup
Preparation time: 5 minutes
Ready time: 5 minutes

Ingredients:
- 1 shot of espresso
- 6 ounces of whole milk
- Optional: sugar or sweetener, to taste

Instructions:
1. Start by brewing a shot of espresso using your preferred method. If you don't have an espresso machine, you can use a Moka pot or a French press to make a strong coffee concentrate.
2. While the espresso is brewing, heat the milk in a small saucepan over medium heat. Stir occasionally to prevent scorching. Heat the milk until it reaches a temperature of around 150°F (65°C). You can use a kitchen thermometer to check the temperature.
3. Once the milk is heated, remove it from the heat and froth it using a milk frother or a handheld frother. The goal is to create microfoam, which is a velvety and creamy texture. Gently tap the frothing pitcher on the counter to remove any large bubbles.
4. Pour the shot of espresso into a cup.
5. Hold the frothing pitcher at a slight angle and pour the milk over the espresso. Start by pouring slowly and then gradually increase the speed. Aim to create a pattern of white foam on top of the coffee.
6. Once you've poured all the milk, use a spoon to scoop out any remaining foam and place it on top of the drink.
7. If desired, add sugar or sweetener to taste.
8. Your Flat White is now ready to be enjoyed!

Nutrition information:
- Calories: 120
- Fat: 6g
- Carbohydrates: 9g
- Protein: 8g
- Sugar: 9g
- Sodium: 100mg

Note: The nutrition information may vary depending on the type of milk and sweetener used.

7. Macchiato

Macchiato is a popular coffee-based beverage that originated in Italy. It is made by combining a shot of espresso with a small amount of steamed milk, creating a delicious and balanced flavor. This drink is perfect for those who enjoy a strong coffee taste with a touch of creaminess.
Serving: 1 Serving: Preparation time: 5 minutes
Ready time: 5 minutes

Ingredients:
- 1 shot of espresso
- 2 ounces of steamed milk
- Optional: caramel or chocolate syrup for garnish

Instructions:
1. Brew a shot of espresso using an espresso machine or a stovetop espresso maker.
2. While the espresso is brewing, heat the milk in a small saucepan over low heat. Alternatively, you can use a milk frother or a microwave to steam the milk until it is hot and frothy.
3. Pour the shot of espresso into a small cup or glass.
4. Gently pour the steamed milk over the espresso, holding back the foam with a spoon to create a layered effect. The milk should create a small "stain" on top of the espresso, hence the name "macchiato," which means "stained" in Italian.
5. If desired, drizzle caramel or chocolate syrup on top for added flavor and decoration.
6. Serve immediately and enjoy!

Nutrition information:
- Calories: 30
- Fat: 1g
- Carbohydrates: 2g
- Protein: 2g
- Sugar: 1g
- Sodium: 30mg
- Caffeine: 63mg

Note: Nutrition information may vary depending on the type and amount of milk used.

8. Affogato

Affogato is an Italian dessert made with espresso and ice cream. It's a creamy and luxurious treat perfect for special occasions.
Serving: 8
Preparation time: 10 minutes
Ready time: 10 minutes

Ingredients:
- 2 cups espresso or strong coffee
- 2 pints of vanilla ice cream
- ½ cup of almonds, chopped
- Whipped cream, for topping
- Chocolate chips, for topping

Instructions:
1. Brew the espresso or strong coffee and let cool.
2. Scoop the ice cream into 8 glasses or dishes.
3. Pour 1/4 cup of the cooled espresso over each scoop of ice cream.
4. Sprinkle the chopped almonds over each glass.
5. Top with whipped cream and chocolate chips.
6. Serve immediately.

Nutrition information: per serving – 375 calories, 27g fat, 36g carbohydrates, 5g protein.

9. Irish Coffee

Irish Coffee is a classic hot beverage that's a combination of hot coffee, whiskey, sugar and cream.
Serving: 1 (8-ounce) cup
Preparation Time: 5 minutes
Ready Time: 10 minutes

Ingredients:
- 1 (8-ounce) cup of freshly brewed hot coffee
- 1 shot of Irish whiskey

- 1 teaspoon of sugar
- Whipped cream

Instructions:
1. Pour the hot coffee into a mug.
2. Add the whiskey and sugar to the coffee and mix.
3. Top with whipped cream and enjoy.

Nutrition information: per serving (8-ounce)
Calories – 195
Fat – 6g
Sodium – 2mg
Carbohydrates – 17g
Protein – 1g

10. Frappuccino

Frappuccino is a blended coffee-based drink that has a creamy and slightly frothy texture made from espresso or stronger coffee, milk, flavored syrups, and ice.
Serving: 4
Preparation Time: 10 minutes
Ready Time: 10 minutes

Ingredients:
- 2 shots of espresso or 4 tablespoons of strong coffee
- 2-3 tablespoons of your preferred sweetner
- 2-3 tablespoons of flavored syrup
- 2 cups of ice
- 1 cup of milk of your choice

Instructions:
1. Put espresso or strong coffee, sweetener and flavored syrup into a blender.
2. Blend for 30 seconds.
3. Add ice and milk, blend for 50-60 seconds.
4. Put the frappuccino into drink glasses and serve.

Nutrition information: Calories 220, Total Fat 3g (Saturated fat 1.5g), Cholesterol 10mg, Sodium 120mg, Total Carbohydrates 40g, Sugars 25g, Protein 8g.

11. Iced Coffee

Iced coffee is a refreshing and energizing beverage that is perfect for those hot summer days or when you need a pick-me-up. Made with freshly brewed coffee and chilled to perfection, this drink is a delightful way to enjoy the rich flavors of coffee in a cool and invigorating way. Whether you're a coffee lover or just looking for a refreshing drink, this iced coffee recipe is sure to satisfy your cravings.
Serving: 1
Preparation time: 5 minutes
Ready time: 10 minutes

Ingredients:
- 1 cup of freshly brewed coffee
- 1 cup of ice cubes
- 2 tablespoons of sugar (adjust according to your preference)
- 1/4 cup of milk (dairy or non-dairy)
- Whipped cream (optional)
- Chocolate syrup or caramel sauce (optional)

Instructions:
1. Brew a cup of coffee using your preferred method. You can use a coffee maker, French press, or any other method you prefer. Make sure the coffee is strong and flavorful.
2. Once the coffee is brewed, let it cool for a few minutes. You can transfer it to a different container and place it in the refrigerator to speed up the cooling process.
3. In a tall glass, add the ice cubes. Pour the cooled coffee over the ice.
4. Add sugar to the glass and stir well until the sugar is completely dissolved. Adjust the amount of sugar according to your taste preferences.
5. Pour the milk into the glass and stir gently to combine with the coffee.
6. If desired, top the iced coffee with whipped cream and drizzle with chocolate syrup or caramel sauce for added indulgence.

7. Give the drink a final stir and serve immediately. Enjoy your homemade iced coffee!

Nutrition information:
- Calories: 70
- Fat: 1g
- Carbohydrates: 15g
- Protein: 1g
- Sugar: 13g
- Sodium: 10mg

Note: The nutrition information may vary depending on the type and amount of Ingredients used.

12. Turkish Coffee

Turkish coffee is a traditional and aromatic beverage that has been enjoyed in Turkey for centuries. It is known for its strong flavor and unique brewing method. This rich and velvety coffee is a perfect way to start your day or enjoy a relaxing afternoon break.

Serving: 1 cup
Preparation time: 5 minutes
Ready time: 10 minutes

Ingredients:
- 1 cup water
- 1 tablespoon Turkish coffee grounds (finely ground)
- Sugar (optional)

Instructions:
1. Start by measuring 1 cup of water and pour it into a small Turkish coffee pot called a cezve.
2. Add 1 tablespoon of Turkish coffee grounds to the water in the cezve. The coffee grounds should be very finely ground, almost like a powder.
3. If you prefer your coffee sweet, you can add sugar to taste at this point. Traditionally, Turkish coffee is served unsweetened, but you can adjust it according to your preference.
4. Place the cezve on the stovetop over low heat. Slowly bring the coffee to a simmer, stirring occasionally with a small spoon.

5. As the coffee begins to heat up, a foam will start to form on the surface. Allow the foam to rise but be careful not to let it boil over.
6. Just before the coffee reaches a boil, remove it from the heat and let it sit for a minute to allow the grounds to settle.
7. Return the cezve to the heat and bring it to a simmer once again. Repeat this process two more times, allowing the foam to rise and removing it from the heat just before it boils.
8. After the third simmer, pour the coffee into a small cup, making sure to leave the settled grounds behind in the cezve.
9. Allow the coffee to sit for a minute or two to let the grounds settle completely.
10. Serve the Turkish coffee hot and enjoy its rich flavor and aroma.

Nutrition information:
- Calories: 5
- Fat: 0g
- Carbohydrates: 1g
- Protein: 0g
- Fiber: 0g
- Sugar: 0g
- Sodium: 0mg

Note: The nutrition information may vary depending on the amount of sugar added.

13. Vietnamese Coffee

Vietnamese Coffee is a unique coffee beverage that incorporates the flavor of sweetened condensed milk to create an indulgent, milky-tasting coffee.
Serving: 2
Preparation Time: 5 minutes
Ready Time: 2 minutes

Ingredients:
- 2 tablespoons of Vietnamese/dark roast ground coffee
- 2 tablespoons of sweetened condensed milk
- 1 cup of water

Instructions:
1. Heat the water until it begins to boil.
2. Place the ground coffee in a coffee filter and place in the Vietnamese filter.
3. Place the filter over a cup and pour the heated water over it.
4. Let it steep for 2 minutes.
5. Add the condensed milk to the cup and stir.
6. Enjoy the Vietnamese Coffee.

Nutrition information:
Calories: 70, Fat: 0.3g, Cholesterol: 4mg, Sodium: 18mg, Carbohydrates: 11g, Sugar: 10g, Protein: 2g.

14. Cortado

Cortado is a popular Spanish coffee beverage that combines equal parts espresso and steamed milk. It is a delicious and balanced drink that is perfect for those who enjoy a strong coffee flavor with a touch of creamy sweetness. Whether you're looking for a morning pick-me-up or a mid-afternoon treat, the cortado is sure to satisfy your coffee cravings.
Serving: 1 cortado
Preparation time: 5 minutes
Ready time: 5 minutes

Ingredients:
- 1 shot of espresso
- 1/2 cup of steamed milk

Instructions:
1. Start by brewing a shot of espresso using your preferred method. If you don't have an espresso machine, you can use a stovetop espresso maker or a French press to make a strong coffee concentrate.
2. While the espresso is brewing, heat the milk in a small saucepan over medium heat. Be careful not to let it boil, as it can scorch and develop a burnt taste. Alternatively, you can use a milk frother or a microwave to steam the milk until it is hot and frothy.
3. Once the espresso is ready, pour it into a small cup or glass.

4. Slowly pour the steamed milk over the espresso, holding back the foam with a spoon to create a 1:1 ratio of espresso to milk.
5. Gently stir the cortado to combine the flavors.
6. Serve immediately and enjoy!

Nutrition information:
- Calories: 60
- Fat: 2g
- Carbohydrates: 6g
- Protein: 4g
- Sugar: 6g
- Sodium: 60mg
- Caffeine: 80mg

Note: Nutrition information may vary depending on the type of milk and espresso used.

15. Breve

Breve is a delicious and creamy coffee-based beverage that is perfect for those who enjoy a rich and indulgent treat. This drink is made by combining espresso with steamed half-and-half, resulting in a smooth and velvety texture that is sure to satisfy your coffee cravings. Whether you enjoy it as a morning pick-me-up or an after-dinner treat, Breve is a delightful way to enjoy the flavors of coffee in a decadent form.

Serving: 1
Preparation time: 5 minutes
Ready time: 5 minutes

Ingredients:
- 1 shot of espresso
- 1 cup of half-and-half
- 1 tablespoon of sugar (optional)
- Whipped cream (optional, for garnish)
- Ground cinnamon or cocoa powder (optional, for garnish)

Instructions:

1. Brew a shot of espresso using your preferred method. If you don't have an espresso machine, you can use a stovetop espresso maker or a French press to make a strong coffee concentrate.
2. In a small saucepan, heat the half-and-half over medium heat until it starts to steam. Be careful not to let it boil.
3. Once the half-and-half is steaming, remove it from the heat and pour it into a blender or use a handheld frother to froth the milk until it becomes creamy and velvety.
4. In a large mug, combine the frothed half-and-half with the shot of espresso. If desired, add sugar to sweeten the drink to your taste.
5. Stir the mixture gently to combine the flavors.
6. If desired, top the Breve with a dollop of whipped cream and sprinkle with ground cinnamon or cocoa powder for an extra touch of indulgence.
7. Serve the Breve immediately and enjoy!

Nutrition information:
- Calories: 180
- Fat: 12g
- Carbohydrates: 12g
- Protein: 6g
- Sugar: 10g
- Sodium: 60mg

Note: The nutrition information provided is an estimate and may vary depending on the specific Ingredients used.

16. Ristretto

Ristretto is a concentrated and intense coffee beverage that originated in Italy. It is made by extracting a small amount of water through finely ground coffee beans, resulting in a strong and flavorful shot of espresso. This rich and aromatic drink is perfect for coffee lovers who enjoy a bold and robust flavor profile.

Serving: 1
Preparation time: 5 minutes
Ready time: 5 minutes

Ingredients:

- 1 shot of espresso (approximately 1 ounce)
- Freshly roasted coffee beans
- Filtered water

Instructions:
1. Start by grinding your coffee beans to a fine consistency. The ideal grind size for a ristretto is slightly finer than that of a regular espresso.
2. Preheat your espresso machine and ensure that it is clean and ready for use.
3. Measure out the desired amount of coffee grounds for a single shot of espresso.
4. Distribute the coffee grounds evenly in the portafilter and tamp them down firmly using a tamper.
5. Lock the portafilter into the espresso machine and place a cup underneath the spout.
6. Start the extraction process and allow the water to flow through the coffee grounds for approximately 20-25 seconds. The resulting shot should be approximately 1 ounce in volume.
7. Once the extraction is complete, remove the cup from under the spout and enjoy your ristretto immediately.

Nutrition information:
- Calories: 0
- Fat: 0g
- Carbohydrates: 0g
- Protein: 0g
- Caffeine content: Approximately 60-75mg per shot

17. Doppio

Doppio is a delicious Italian coffee beverage that is perfect for those who love a strong and bold flavor. This double shot of espresso is a popular choice among coffee enthusiasts and is often enjoyed as a morning pick-me-up or an afternoon treat. With its rich and intense taste, Doppio is sure to satisfy any coffee lover's cravings.
Serving: 1
Preparation time: 5 minutes
Ready time: 5 minutes

Ingredients:
- 2 ounces of freshly brewed espresso
- Hot water (optional, for Americano-style Doppio)
- Sugar or sweetener (optional, to taste)

Instructions:
1. Start by brewing a double shot of espresso using your espresso machine. This will yield approximately 2 ounces of espresso. If you don't have an espresso machine, you can use a stovetop espresso maker or a French press to make a strong coffee concentrate.
2. If you prefer a milder flavor, you can dilute the espresso with hot water to make an Americano-style Doppio. Simply add hot water to the espresso until you reach your desired strength.
3. If desired, add sugar or sweetener to taste. Stir well to dissolve the sugar.
4. Serve the Doppio in a small espresso cup or a demitasse. Enjoy it as is or pair it with a biscotti or a small pastry for a delightful treat.

Nutrition information:
- Calories: 0
- Fat: 0g
- Carbohydrates: 0g
- Protein: 0g
- Caffeine: Approximately 150mg (may vary depending on the type of coffee beans used)

18. Lungo

Lungo is a delicious and aromatic Italian coffee beverage that is perfect for those who enjoy a longer and stronger cup of coffee. This recipe will guide you through the process of making a perfect Lungo at home, allowing you to savor the rich flavors and smooth texture of this classic drink.

Serving: 1 cup
Preparation time: 5 minutes
Ready time: 10 minutes

Ingredients:
- 1 Lungo coffee capsule or 2 tablespoons of finely ground coffee
- 6 ounces of hot water
- Sugar or sweetener (optional)
- Milk or cream (optional)

Instructions:
1. Start by heating the water until it reaches a temperature of around 200°F (93°C). You can use a kettle or heat the water on the stovetop.
2. While the water is heating, prepare your Lungo coffee capsule by placing it in the coffee machine or espresso maker. If you are using ground coffee, make sure it is finely ground for optimal extraction.
3. Once the water is heated, pour it slowly over the coffee grounds or capsule. Make sure to pour in a circular motion to ensure even extraction.
4. Allow the coffee to brew for approximately 1-2 minutes, or until the desired strength is achieved. The longer the brewing time, the stronger the flavor will be.
5. Once the brewing is complete, remove the coffee capsule or strain the coffee grounds using a fine-mesh sieve.
6. If desired, add sugar or sweetener to taste. You can also add milk or cream for a creamier taste.
7. Stir well to combine all the Ingredients and enjoy your homemade Lungo!

Nutrition information:
- Calories: 0
- Fat: 0g
- Carbohydrates: 0g
- Protein: 0g
- Fiber: 0g
- Sugar: 0g
- Sodium: 0mg

Please note that the nutrition information may vary depending on the specific brand of coffee used and any additional Ingredients you choose to add.

19. Espresso Martini

The Espresso Martini is a delightful cocktail that combines the rich flavors of espresso with the smoothness of vodka. It is the perfect drink for coffee lovers who also enjoy a little kick of alcohol. This cocktail is not only delicious but also easy to make, making it a great choice for any occasion.

Serving: 1 cocktail
Preparation time: 5 minutes
Ready time: 5 minutes

Ingredients:
- 1 shot of espresso (30ml)
- 1 shot of vodka (30ml)
- 1 shot of coffee liqueur (30ml)
- 1 teaspoon of simple syrup
- Ice cubes
- Coffee beans (for garnish)

Instructions:
1. Brew a shot of espresso and let it cool down to room temperature.
2. Fill a cocktail shaker with ice cubes.
3. Add the shot of espresso, vodka, coffee liqueur, and simple syrup to the shaker.
4. Shake vigorously for about 15 seconds to combine all the Ingredients and chill the cocktail.
5. Strain the mixture into a chilled martini glass.
6. Garnish with a few coffee beans on top.
7. Serve and enjoy!

Nutrition information:
- Calories: 180
- Fat: 0g
- Carbohydrates: 12g
- Protein: 0g
- Sugar: 12g
- Sodium: 0mg
- Fiber: 0g

Note: The nutrition information may vary depending on the specific brands of Ingredients used.

20. Pumpkin Spice Latte

Pumpkin Spice Latte is a delicious and cozy fall beverage that combines the flavors of pumpkin, warm spices, and creamy milk. This comforting drink is perfect for chilly mornings or as an afternoon treat. With just a few simple Ingredients, you can easily make this popular coffee shop favorite at home.
Serving: 1 Serving: Preparation time: 5 minutes
Ready time: 10 minutes

Ingredients:
- 1 cup milk (any type you prefer, such as whole, almond, or oat milk)
- 1/4 cup pumpkin puree
- 1 tablespoon sugar (adjust according to your taste)
- 1/2 teaspoon pumpkin pie spice
- 1/2 teaspoon vanilla extract
- 1/2 cup strong brewed coffee or 1 shot of espresso
- Whipped cream (optional)
- Ground cinnamon or nutmeg for garnish (optional)

Instructions:
1. In a small saucepan, heat the milk over medium heat until hot but not boiling. Stir occasionally to prevent scorching.
2. In a separate bowl, whisk together the pumpkin puree, sugar, pumpkin pie spice, and vanilla extract until well combined.
3. Add the pumpkin mixture to the hot milk and whisk until smooth and heated through.
4. If using brewed coffee, pour it into a mug. If using espresso, add the shot directly to the mug.
5. Slowly pour the pumpkin milk mixture over the coffee, stirring gently to combine.
6. Top with whipped cream if desired and sprinkle with ground cinnamon or nutmeg for an extra touch of flavor.
7. Serve hot and enjoy!

Nutrition information:
- Calories: 150

- Fat: 4g
- Carbohydrates: 25g
- Protein: 6g
- Fiber: 2g
- Sugar: 20g
- Sodium: 100mg

Note: Nutrition information may vary depending on the type of milk and sugar used.

21. Hazelnut Latte

Hazelnut Latte is a warm and comforting drink espresso-based drink made with steamed milk, espresso, and creamy hazelnut syrup. Enjoy this classic Italian Café favorite any time of day!
Serving: 1
Preparation time: 2 minutes
Ready time: 3 minutes

Ingredients:
- 2 ounces espresso
- 2 tablespoons hazelnut syrup
- 6 ounces steamed milk

Instructions:
1. Make the espresso shot and combine it with the hazelnut syrup.
2. Heat the steamed milk in a mug and pour the espresso-hazelnut mixture over it.
3. Stir and enjoy.

Nutrition information:
Calories: 150 kcal, Carbohydrates: 24 g, Protein: 8 g, Fat: 3 g, Sodium: 178 mg, Potassium: 199 mg, Sugar: 19 g.

22. Vanilla Latte

Vanila Latte is a delicious and creamy coffee beverage that is perfect for those who enjoy a hint of sweetness in their coffee. Enjoy this simple

and easy to make latte that is an upgrade from a regular cup of brewed coffee.
Serving: 1
Preparation Time: 5 minutes
Ready Time: 5 minutes

Ingredients:
- 3/4 cup freshly brewed espresso or very strong coffee
- 1 cup milk (dairy or non-dairy)
- 2 tablespoons vanilla flavoring syrup

Instructions:
1. Start by preparing the espresso or strong coffee according to the instructions, and set aside
2. Steam the milk until it starts to foam.
3. Pour the espresso into a mug, and add the vanilla flavoring syrup.
4. Pour the steamed milk into the mug and stir.
5. Serve and enjoy!

Nutrition information Per Serving: Calories: 150
Fat: 4 g
Carbohydrates: 17 g
Protein: 7 g

23. Caramel Macchiato

Caramel Macchiato is a delicious and indulgent coffee-based beverage that combines the rich flavors of espresso, caramel, and milk. This creamy and sweet drink is perfect for those who enjoy a little bit of luxury in their daily coffee routine. Whether you want to treat yourself or impress your guests, this recipe will guide you through creating a homemade Caramel Macchiato that rivals any coffee shop version.
Serving: 1 Serving: Preparation time: 5 minutes
Ready time: 5 minutes

Ingredients:
- 1 shot of espresso (or 1/2 cup of strong brewed coffee)
- 1 cup of milk

- 2 tablespoons of caramel sauce
- 1 tablespoon of vanilla syrup
- Whipped cream (optional)
- Caramel drizzle (optional)

Instructions:
1. Brew a shot of espresso using an espresso machine or make a strong cup of coffee using your preferred method. Set aside.
2. In a small saucepan, heat the milk over medium heat until it starts to steam. Do not let it boil.
3. While the milk is heating, pour the caramel sauce and vanilla syrup into a coffee mug.
4. Once the milk is steaming, carefully pour it into the mug over the caramel sauce and vanilla syrup. Use a spoon to stir until the caramel sauce is fully dissolved.
5. Pour the shot of espresso or strong brewed coffee into the mug, gently pouring it over the back of a spoon to create a layered effect.
6. If desired, top the Caramel Macchiato with whipped cream and a drizzle of caramel sauce.
7. Serve immediately and enjoy!

Nutrition information:
- Calories: 200
- Fat: 6g
- Carbohydrates: 30g
- Protein: 8g
- Sugar: 25g
- Sodium: 120mg

Note: Nutrition information may vary depending on the specific brands and quantities of Ingredients used.

24. White Chocolate Mocha

White Chocolate Mocha is a sweet and creamy combination of white chocolate and espresso. It's a classic favorite for those looking for a special treat.
Serving: 1
Preparation Time: 8 minutes

Ready Time: 8 minutes

Ingredients:
- 2 shots of double-strength espresso
- 2 tablespoons of white chocolate chips
- 2 tablespoons of heavy cream
- Sugar (optional)

Instructions:
1. Prepare the double-strength espresso shots according to the manufacturer's directions.
2. Add the white chocolate chips to a mug and pour the hot espresso over them. Stir until the chips are completely melted.
3. Add the heavy cream and stir to combine.
4. Taste the mocha and add sugar if desired.
5. Serve hot.

Nutrition information:
Calories: 170, Total Fat: 9g, Saturated Fat: 5g, Monounsaturated Fat: 2g, Cholesterol: 8mg, Sodium: 11mg, Potassium: 95mg, Carbohydrates: 21g, Dietary Fiber: 0g, Sugars: 17g, Protein: 3g.

25. Peppermint Mocha

Warm up with a delicious peppermint mocha, a creamy and chocolaty espresso drink blended with peppermint essences.
Serving: 2
Preparation Time: 5 minutes
Ready Time: 5 minutes

Ingredients:
- 2 shots of espresso
- 1 cup of milk
- 2 tablespoons of cocoa powder
- 2 drops of peppermint extract
- 2-3 tablespoons of sugar
- Whipped cream (optional)

Instructions:
1. Start by preparing 2 shots of espresso
2. Pour the espresso into a heat-resistant cup
3. Add the cocoa powder, peppermint extract, and sugar to the coffee and stir
4. In a microwave-safe bowl, add the milk and heat on high for 40 seconds
5. Pour the heated milk into the cup with the coffee mixture and stir
6. Add the whipped cream (optional) and stir
7. Enjoy your peppermint mocha!

Nutrition information:
Calories: 129, Protein: 6g, Carbohydrates: 13g, Fat: 5g, Sodium: 67mg, Cholesterol: 13mg

26. Coconut Mocha

Coconut Mocha is a delightful and indulgent beverage that combines the rich flavors of coconut and chocolate with a hint of coffee. This creamy and aromatic drink is perfect for those who love the combination of tropical and chocolatey flavors. Whether you enjoy it as a morning pick-me-up or as an after-dinner treat, Coconut Mocha is sure to satisfy your cravings.
Serving: 1 Serving: Preparation time: 5 minutes
Ready time: 10 minutes

Ingredients:
- 1 cup of brewed coffee
- 1/2 cup of coconut milk
- 2 tablespoons of cocoa powder
- 2 tablespoons of sugar
- 1/4 teaspoon of vanilla extract
- Whipped cream (optional)
- Shredded coconut (optional)

Instructions:
1. In a small saucepan, heat the coconut milk over medium heat until it starts to simmer. Do not let it boil.

2. In a separate bowl, whisk together the cocoa powder and sugar until well combined.
3. Slowly pour the hot coconut milk into the cocoa powder mixture, whisking constantly to create a smooth and creamy consistency.
4. Add the brewed coffee and vanilla extract to the mixture, stirring well to combine all the flavors.
5. Pour the Coconut Mocha into a mug and top with whipped cream and shredded coconut, if desired.
6. Serve hot and enjoy!

Nutrition information:
- Calories: 150
- Fat: 8g
- Carbohydrates: 18g
- Protein: 2g
- Fiber: 3g
- Sugar: 12g
- Sodium: 20mg

Note: Nutrition information may vary depending on the specific brands and quantities of Ingredients used.

27. Almond Milk Latte

Enjoy the delicious combination of silky almond milk, creamy espresso, and fragrant cinnamon in this Almond Milk Latte. Sweet enough for a dessert, but guilt-free enough to enjoy any time of day!

Serving: 1
Preparation time: 5 minutes
Ready time: 5 minutes

Ingredients:
- 2 shots espresso
- 2 tablespoons almond butter
- 2 tablespoons agave syrup
- ¼ teaspoon ground cinnamon
- 2 cups unsweetened almond milk

Instructions:

1. Brew 2 shots of espresso using an espresso machine.
2. In a blender, combine the espresso, almond butter, agave syrup, and cinnamon and blend until smooth.
3. Pour into a saucepan and whisk in the almond milk. Heat the mixture over medium heat for 5 minutes, whisking frequently.
4. Serve the latte in a mug. Optional: sprinkle the top with additional ground cinnamon for a touch of extra flavor.

Nutrition information: Per serving: Calories: 234, Fat: 10.2g, Saturated fat: 1.6g, Carbohydrates: 28.6g, Sugar: 24.9g, Sodium: 120.1mg, Fiber: 1.5g, Protein: 7.3g

28. Soy Milk Latte

Soy Milk Latte is a delicious variation of the classic latte drink, made with soy milk for a hint of nutty flavor. It is light and creamy, making it a great choice for a soothing morning drink.
Serving: Makes two (2) 8-ounce servings
Preparation time: 5 minutes
Ready time: 5 minutes

Ingredients:
- 1 cup hot strongly brewed coffee
- 2 tablespoons of sugar to taste
- 2 tablespoons of finely ground espresso
- 2 cups unsweetened soy milk
- A sprinkle of cinnamon

Instructions:
1. In a blender, combine hot coffee, sugar, espresso, and soy milk.
2. Blend on high for about 1 minute, or until mixture is foamy.
3. Divide coffee mixture evenly between two mugs.
4. Sprinkle a light dusting of cinnamon on top of each latte.
5. Serve warm and enjoy!

Nutrition information: Calories: 130, Fat: 3 g, Carbohydrates: 17 g, Protein: 8 g, Sodium: 135 mg

29. Oat Milk Latte

Oat Milk Latte is a delicious and creamy alternative to traditional dairy-based lattes. Made with oat milk, this latte is not only dairy-free but also packed with nutrients. It's the perfect way to start your day or enjoy as an afternoon pick-me-up.

Serving: 1 Serving: Preparation time: 5 minutes
Ready time: 10 minutes

Ingredients:
- 1 cup oat milk
- 1 shot of espresso or 1/2 cup of strong brewed coffee
- 1 tablespoon maple syrup or sweetener of your choice
- 1/2 teaspoon vanilla extract
- Ground cinnamon or cocoa powder for garnish (optional)

Instructions:
1. In a small saucepan, heat the oat milk over medium heat until hot but not boiling.
2. While the milk is heating, brew a shot of espresso or make a strong cup of coffee.
3. Once the oat milk is hot, remove it from the heat and whisk vigorously until frothy. You can also use a milk frother if you have one.
4. In a mug, combine the hot espresso or coffee, maple syrup, and vanilla extract. Stir well to combine.
5. Slowly pour the frothy oat milk into the mug, holding back the foam with a spoon to create a layered effect.
6. Sprinkle with ground cinnamon or cocoa powder if desired.
7. Serve immediately and enjoy!

Nutrition information:
- Calories: 120
- Fat: 3g
- Carbohydrates: 20g
- Protein: 2g
- Fiber: 2g
- Sugar: 10g
- Sodium: 80mg

Note: Nutrition information may vary depending on the brand of oat milk and sweetener used.

30. Cold Brew

Cold brew is a refreshing and smooth coffee beverage that is perfect for hot summer days or anytime you need a pick-me-up. Unlike traditional hot brewed coffee, cold brew is made by steeping coffee grounds in cold water for an extended period of time, resulting in a less acidic and more concentrated flavor. With just a few simple Ingredients and a little patience, you can enjoy a delicious cup of cold brew at home.
Serving: 1 cup
Preparation time: 10 minutes (plus 12-24 hours steeping time)
Ready time: 12-24 hours

Ingredients:
- 1 cup coarsely ground coffee beans
- 4 cups cold water
- Optional: milk, sweetener, or flavorings of your choice

Instructions:
1. In a large jar or pitcher, combine the coarsely ground coffee beans and cold water. Stir gently to ensure all the coffee grounds are fully saturated.
2. Cover the jar or pitcher with a lid or plastic wrap and let it steep in the refrigerator for 12-24 hours. The longer you steep, the stronger and more concentrated the cold brew will be.
3. After the steeping time is complete, strain the cold brew through a fine-mesh sieve or a coffee filter to remove the coffee grounds. You can also use a French press for this step if you have one.
4. If desired, dilute the cold brew with water or milk to your preferred strength. Add sweetener or flavorings, such as vanilla extract or caramel syrup, if desired.
5. Serve the cold brew over ice and enjoy! You can store any leftover cold brew in the refrigerator for up to one week.

Nutrition information per serving (without milk or sweeteners):
- Calories: 0
- Fat: 0g

- Carbohydrates: 0g
- Protein: 0g
- Sodium: 0mg
- Sugar: 0g

Note: The nutrition information may vary depending on the type and amount of milk or sweeteners added.

31. Nitro Cold Brew

Nitro Cold Brew is a cold coffee drink infused with nitrogen gas to give it a creamier and more velvety texture. It's easy to make at home and is a great treat for those who love cold coffee.

Serving: 2 cups
Preparation Time: 5 minutes
Ready Time: 10 minutes

Ingredients:
- Freshly-brewed coffee – 3 cups
- Nitrogen – ¼ cup
- Ice cubes – ¼ cup
- Sugar (optional) – to taste

Instructions:
1. Start by making a fresh batch of coffee and pour it into a sealed container.
2. When the coffee has cooled, add in the nitrogen and mix it in well.
3. Pour the coffee into two glasses over ice cubes and stir to combine.
4. If desired, sweeten with sugar and serve immediately.

Nutrition information: Serving size of 2 cups, 1g of fat, 6g of carbohydrate, 0g of protein.

32. Iced Caramel Macchiato

Iced Caramel Macchiato is a refreshing and indulgent coffee-based beverage that combines the rich flavors of caramel and espresso with a creamy milk base. This delightful drink is perfect for those hot summer

days when you need a pick-me-up that also satisfies your sweet tooth. With just a few simple Ingredients and easy steps, you can enjoy this delicious treat in the comfort of your own home.
Serving: 1
Preparation time: 5 minutes
Ready time: 10 minutes

Ingredients:
- 1 shot of espresso or 1/2 cup of strong brewed coffee
- 1 cup of milk (any type you prefer, such as whole, skim, almond, or soy)
- 2 tablespoons of caramel syrup
- 1 cup of ice cubes
- Whipped cream (optional)
- Caramel drizzle (optional)

Instructions:
1. Brew a shot of espresso or make a strong cup of coffee using your preferred method. Allow it to cool for a few minutes.
2. In a glass, add the caramel syrup and swirl it around to coat the sides.
3. Fill the glass with ice cubes.
4. Pour the cooled espresso or coffee over the ice.
5. In a separate container, heat the milk until hot but not boiling. You can use a microwave or stovetop for this step.
6. Froth the milk using a frother or by vigorously shaking it in a sealed container until it becomes creamy and frothy.
7. Pour the frothed milk over the espresso or coffee and ice.
8. Stir gently to combine all the Ingredients.
9. If desired, top with whipped cream and drizzle some caramel syrup on top for an extra indulgent touch.
10. Serve immediately and enjoy!

Nutrition information:
- Calories: 180
- Fat: 6g
- Carbohydrates: 25g
- Protein: 8g
- Sugar: 20g
- Sodium: 120mg

Note: Nutrition information may vary depending on the type of milk and caramel syrup used.

33. Iced Vanilla Latte

Iced Vanilla Latte is a refreshing and creamy coffee beverage that is perfect for those hot summer days or when you need a pick-me-up. This delightful drink combines the rich flavors of coffee and vanilla, creating a smooth and indulgent treat. Whether you enjoy it in the morning or as an afternoon pick-me-up, this Iced Vanilla Latte is sure to satisfy your coffee cravings.

Serving: 1
Preparation time: 5 minutes
Ready time: 5 minutes

Ingredients:
- 1 cup of strong brewed coffee, chilled
- 1 cup of milk (dairy or non-dairy)
- 2 tablespoons of vanilla syrup
- Ice cubes
- Whipped cream (optional)
- Ground cinnamon or cocoa powder for garnish (optional)

Instructions:
1. Brew a cup of strong coffee using your preferred method. Allow it to cool completely or refrigerate until chilled.
2. In a glass, combine the chilled coffee, milk, and vanilla syrup. Stir well to ensure the syrup is evenly distributed.
3. Fill a separate glass with ice cubes.
4. Pour the coffee mixture over the ice cubes, filling the glass to the top.
5. If desired, top with whipped cream and sprinkle with ground cinnamon or cocoa powder for an extra touch of flavor.
6. Stir gently to combine the flavors and enjoy your refreshing Iced Vanilla Latte!

Nutrition information:
- Calories: 150
- Fat: 4g

- Carbohydrates: 25g
- Protein: 5g
- Sugar: 20g
- Sodium: 80mg
- Fiber: 0g

Note: Nutrition information may vary depending on the type of milk and vanilla syrup used.

34. Iced Matcha Latte

Iced Matcha Latte is a refreshing and energizing drink that combines the earthy flavors of matcha green tea with the creamy goodness of milk. This delightful beverage is perfect for hot summer days or as a pick-me-up any time of the year. With its vibrant green color and smooth texture, it's not only delicious but also visually appealing. Give this recipe a try and enjoy the invigorating taste of matcha in a cool and creamy form.
Serving: 1
Preparation time: 5 minutes
Ready time: 10 minutes

Ingredients:
- 1 teaspoon matcha green tea powder
- 1 tablespoon hot water
- 1 cup milk (dairy or plant-based)
- 1 tablespoon honey or sweetener of choice (optional)
- Ice cubes

Instructions:
1. In a small bowl, whisk the matcha green tea powder with hot water until it forms a smooth paste. Make sure there are no lumps.
2. In a separate glass or jar, add the milk and sweetener (if using). Stir well to combine.
3. Pour the matcha paste into the milk mixture and stir until fully incorporated.
4. Fill a glass with ice cubes and pour the matcha latte over the ice.
5. Stir gently to chill the drink and ensure the matcha is evenly distributed.

6. Taste and adjust sweetness if desired by adding more honey or sweetener.
7. Serve immediately and enjoy the refreshing Iced Matcha Latte!

Nutrition information:
- Calories: 120
- Fat: 4g
- Carbohydrates: 15g
- Protein: 8g
- Fiber: 1g
- Sugar: 12g
- Sodium: 100mg

Note: Nutrition information may vary depending on the type of milk and sweetener used.

35. Iced Chai Latte

Iced Chai Latte is a refreshing and flavorful beverage that combines the rich and aromatic flavors of chai tea with the creamy goodness of milk. This chilled drink is perfect for hot summer days or as a pick-me-up any time of the year. With just a few simple Ingredients and easy steps, you can enjoy a delicious Iced Chai Latte in no time.

Serving: 1
Preparation time: 5 minutes
Ready time: 10 minutes

Ingredients:
- 1 chai tea bag
- 1 cup water
- 1 cup milk (dairy or non-dairy)
- 1 tablespoon honey or sweetener of your choice (optional)
- Ice cubes

Instructions:
1. In a small saucepan, bring the water to a boil.
2. Add the chai tea bag to the boiling water and let it steep for 5 minutes.
3. Remove the tea bag and let the chai tea cool to room temperature.
4. Once the chai tea has cooled, pour it into a glass filled with ice cubes.

5. In a separate saucepan, heat the milk over medium heat until hot but not boiling.
6. Pour the hot milk over the chai tea and ice cubes in the glass.
7. Stir in honey or sweetener if desired.
8. Give the Iced Chai Latte a good stir to combine all the flavors.
9. Serve immediately and enjoy!

Nutrition information:
- Calories: 120
- Fat: 4g
- Carbohydrates: 18g
- Protein: 5g
- Sugar: 14g
- Fiber: 1g

Note: Nutrition information may vary depending on the type of milk and sweetener used.

36. Iced Coconut Mocha

This delicious Iced Coconut Mocha is the perfect mid-day pick-me-up. Made with espresso, coconut milk, and chocolate, this beverage is sure to satisfy.
Serving: Makes one drink.
Preparation Time: 5 minutes
Ready Time: 5 minutes

Ingredients:
- 1 shot of espresso
- ½ cup of coconut milk
- 2 tsp cocoa powder
- 1 tsp granulated sugar
- Ice

Instructions:
1. Brew 1 shot of espresso.
2. In a small bowl, whisk together cocoa powder, sugar, and coconut milk until frothy.
3. Fill a 12-ounce glass with ice.

4. Pour espresso over the ice.
5. Slowly pour chocolate-coconut mixture over the espresso.
6. Serve and enjoy!

Nutrition information (per serving):
- Calories: 123
- Fat: 8.3 g
- Carbs: 9.9 g
- Protein: 1.8 g

37. Iced Hazelnut Latte

Iced Hazelnut Latte is a refreshing and indulgent coffee beverage that combines the rich flavors of hazelnut and the smoothness of a latte. This chilled drink is perfect for those hot summer days when you need a pick-me-up that will also cool you down. With just a few simple Ingredients, you can easily make this delicious treat at home and enjoy it whenever you crave a creamy and nutty coffee experience.

Serving: 1
Preparation time: 5 minutes
Ready time: 10 minutes

Ingredients:
- 1 cup of strong brewed coffee, chilled
- 1 cup of milk (dairy or plant-based)
- 2 tablespoons of hazelnut syrup
- 1 tablespoon of sugar (optional)
- Ice cubes
- Whipped cream (optional)
- Crushed hazelnuts (optional)

Instructions:
1. Brew a cup of strong coffee using your preferred method. Allow it to cool completely or refrigerate until chilled.
2. In a glass, combine the chilled coffee, milk, hazelnut syrup, and sugar (if desired). Stir well to ensure the syrup and sugar are fully dissolved.
3. Fill a separate glass with ice cubes. Pour the coffee mixture over the ice, leaving some room at the top for additional toppings.

4. If desired, top the drink with a dollop of whipped cream and a sprinkle of crushed hazelnuts for added flavor and presentation.
5. Give the iced hazelnut latte a gentle stir to mix in the toppings and enjoy immediately.

Nutrition information:
- Calories: 150
- Fat: 5g
- Carbohydrates: 20g
- Protein: 5g
- Sugar: 15g
- Fiber: 1g

Note: The nutrition information provided is an estimate and may vary depending on the specific Ingredients and brands used.

38. Iced Almond Milk Latte

Iced Almond Milk Latte is a refreshing and dairy-free alternative to traditional lattes. Made with smooth almond milk and a shot of espresso, this drink is perfect for those looking for a lighter and healthier coffee option. With its creamy texture and nutty flavor, it's sure to become your new favorite summer beverage.

Serving: 1
Preparation time: 5 minutes
Ready time: 5 minutes

Ingredients:
- 1 cup almond milk
- 1 shot of espresso (or 1/2 cup of strong brewed coffee)
- 1 tablespoon sweetener of your choice (such as honey, maple syrup, or agave nectar)
- Ice cubes

Instructions:
1. In a glass, add ice cubes until it's about 3/4 full.
2. In a separate container, heat the almond milk until warm. You can do this on the stovetop or in the microwave.
3. Pour the warm almond milk over the ice cubes in the glass.

4. Brew a shot of espresso or make a strong cup of coffee using your preferred method.
5. Add the shot of espresso or coffee to the glass with almond milk and ice.
6. Stir in your desired sweetener until it's well combined.
7. Give the drink a good stir to mix all the Ingredients together.
8. Add more ice if desired and enjoy your Iced Almond Milk Latte!

Nutrition information:
- Calories: 60
- Fat: 2g
- Carbohydrates: 9g
- Protein: 1g
- Sugar: 7g
- Fiber: 1g

Note: Nutrition information may vary depending on the brand of almond milk and sweetener used.

39. Iced Soy Milk Latte

Iced Soy Milk Latte is a refreshing and dairy-free alternative to traditional iced lattes. Made with smooth and creamy soy milk, this beverage is perfect for those who are lactose intolerant or following a vegan lifestyle. With a hint of sweetness and a bold coffee flavor, this iced latte is sure to become your new favorite summer drink.

Serving: 1
Preparation time: 5 minutes
Ready time: 5 minutes

Ingredients:
- 1 cup of soy milk
- 1 shot of espresso or 1/2 cup of strong brewed coffee
- 1 tablespoon of sweetener (such as agave syrup or maple syrup)
- Ice cubes

Instructions:
1. Brew a shot of espresso or make a strong cup of coffee using your preferred method. Allow it to cool for a few minutes.

2. In a glass, add ice cubes until it's about 3/4 full.
3. Pour the cooled espresso or coffee over the ice cubes.
4. In a separate container, heat the soy milk until warm. You can use a microwave or stovetop for this step.
5. Once the soy milk is warm, froth it using a frother or whisk until it becomes creamy and frothy.
6. Pour the frothed soy milk over the espresso or coffee in the glass.
7. Add the sweetener of your choice and stir well to combine all the Ingredients.
8. Add more ice cubes if desired and serve immediately.

Nutrition information:
- Calories: 100
- Fat: 4g
- Carbohydrates: 12g
- Protein: 6g
- Fiber: 1g
- Sugar: 8g
- Sodium: 80mg

Note: Nutrition information may vary depending on the brand of soy milk and sweetener used.

40. Iced Oat Milk Latte

Iced Oat Milk Latte is a refreshing and dairy-free alternative to traditional lattes. Made with creamy oat milk and a shot of espresso, this drink is perfect for those looking for a delicious and energizing pick-me-up. With its smooth and velvety texture, it's sure to become your new favorite summer beverage.

Serving: 1
Preparation time: 5 minutes
Ready time: 5 minutes

Ingredients:
- 1 cup oat milk
- 1 shot of espresso (or 1/2 cup strong brewed coffee)
- 1 tablespoon maple syrup (optional)
- Ice cubes

Instructions:
1. In a glass, add ice cubes until it's about 3/4 full.
2. Pour the oat milk over the ice cubes, leaving some space at the top for the espresso.
3. If desired, add the maple syrup for a touch of sweetness.
4. Brew a shot of espresso or prepare 1/2 cup of strong brewed coffee.
5. Pour the espresso or coffee over the oat milk and ice.
6. Stir gently to combine all the Ingredients.
7. Serve immediately and enjoy your refreshing Iced Oat Milk Latte!

Nutrition information:
- Calories: 120
- Fat: 3g
- Carbohydrates: 20g
- Protein: 2g
- Fiber: 1g
- Sugar: 10g
- Sodium: 80mg

Note: Nutrition information may vary depending on the brand of oat milk and optional Ingredients used.

41. Espresso Con Panna

Espresso Con Panna is a delightful Italian coffee-based beverage that is perfect for those who enjoy a rich and creamy treat. This indulgent drink combines the bold flavors of espresso with a dollop of whipped cream, creating a harmonious balance of bitterness and sweetness. Whether you're looking for a pick-me-up in the morning or a luxurious after-dinner treat, Espresso Con Panna is sure to satisfy your coffee cravings.
Serving: 1 Serving: Preparation time: 5 minutes
Ready time: 5 minutes

Ingredients:
- 1 shot of espresso
- 2 tablespoons of whipped cream
- Cocoa powder or chocolate shavings (optional, for garnish)

Instructions:
1. Brew a shot of espresso using your preferred method. If you don't have an espresso machine, you can use a stovetop Moka pot or a French press to make a strong coffee concentrate.
2. While the espresso is brewing, whip the cream until it reaches a soft peak consistency. You can use an electric mixer or whisk it by hand.
3. Once the espresso is ready, pour it into a small espresso cup or a heatproof glass.
4. Spoon the whipped cream on top of the espresso, creating a generous dollop.
5. If desired, sprinkle some cocoa powder or chocolate shavings over the whipped cream for an extra touch of decadence.
6. Serve immediately and enjoy the rich flavors of Espresso Con Panna.

Nutrition information:
- Calories: 60
- Fat: 5g
- Carbohydrates: 1g
- Protein: 1g
- Sugar: 0g
- Sodium: 10mg
- Caffeine: 63mg

Note: The nutrition information provided is an estimate and may vary depending on the specific Ingredients and brands used.

42. Vienna Coffee

Vienna Coffee is a classic coffee beverage that originated in Vienna, Austria. It is a delightful combination of strong coffee, whipped cream, and a touch of chocolate. This rich and indulgent drink is perfect for those who enjoy a little sweetness in their coffee. Whether you want to start your day with a special treat or enjoy a cozy afternoon pick-me-up, Vienna Coffee is sure to satisfy your cravings.

Serving: 1 cup
Preparation time: 5 minutes
Ready time: 10 minutes

Ingredients:

- 1 cup strong brewed coffee
- 2 tablespoons granulated sugar
- 2 tablespoons heavy cream
- 1 tablespoon chocolate syrup
- Whipped cream, for topping
- Cocoa powder or chocolate shavings, for garnish (optional)

Instructions:
1. Brew a cup of strong coffee using your preferred method. You can use an espresso machine, a French press, or a drip coffee maker.
2. In a small saucepan, heat the heavy cream over low heat until it starts to steam. Do not let it boil.
3. Add the sugar to the hot coffee and stir until it dissolves completely.
4. Pour the hot coffee into a mug, leaving some space at the top for the whipped cream.
5. Slowly pour the steamed heavy cream over the back of a spoon into the coffee. This will create a layered effect.
6. Drizzle the chocolate syrup over the whipped cream.
7. Top with a generous dollop of whipped cream.
8. If desired, sprinkle some cocoa powder or chocolate shavings on top for an extra touch of decadence.
9. Serve immediately and enjoy!

Nutrition information:
- Calories: 150
- Fat: 8g
- Carbohydrates: 18g
- Protein: 1g
- Sugar: 16g
- Sodium: 10mg
- Fiber: 0g

Note: The nutrition information is approximate and may vary depending on the specific brands and quantities of Ingredients used.

43. Caramel Cappuccino

Indulge in the rich and creamy flavors of a Caramel Cappuccino, a delightful coffee-based beverage that will awaken your senses and satisfy your sweet tooth. This recipe combines the smoothness of a classic cappuccino with the irresistible sweetness of caramel, creating a perfect balance of flavors. Whether you enjoy it as a morning pick-me-up or a cozy evening treat, this Caramel Cappuccino is sure to become your new favorite coffee drink.

Serving: 1 cup
Preparation time: 5 minutes
Ready time: 10 minutes

Ingredients:
- 1 shot of espresso or 1/2 cup of strong brewed coffee
- 1 cup of milk
- 2 tablespoons of caramel syrup
- 1/4 teaspoon of vanilla extract
- Whipped cream (optional)
- Caramel sauce for drizzling (optional)

Instructions:
1. Brew a shot of espresso or make a strong cup of coffee using your preferred method.
2. In a small saucepan, heat the milk over medium heat until it starts to steam. Do not let it boil.
3. While the milk is heating, pour the caramel syrup into a mug.
4. Once the milk is steaming, remove it from the heat and whisk vigorously for about 30 seconds to create froth.
5. Pour the hot milk over the caramel syrup in the mug, holding back the froth with a spoon.
6. Add the shot of espresso or brewed coffee to the mug, followed by the vanilla extract. Stir gently to combine all the flavors.
7. If desired, top the Caramel Cappuccino with a dollop of whipped cream and drizzle some caramel sauce on top for an extra touch of indulgence.
8. Serve immediately and enjoy the rich and creamy goodness of your homemade Caramel Cappuccino.

Nutrition information:
- Calories: 150
- Fat: 4g
- Carbohydrates: 25g
- Protein: 6g

- Sugar: 20g
- Sodium: 100mg

Note: Nutrition information may vary depending on the specific brands and quantities of Ingredients used.

44. White Mocha Latte

White Mocha Latte is an aromatic and delectable coffee-based beverage that combines rich espresso with frothy milk and sweet white chocolate.
Serving: 1
Preparation Time: 5 minutes
Ready Time: 5 minutes

Ingredients:
- 2 ounces of espresso
- 2 ounces of white chocolate syrup
- 2 cups of steamed milk

Instructions:
1. Brew espresso into a cup.
2. Add 2 ounces of white chocolate syrup.
3. Froth 2 cups of steamed milk, and add the foam to the espresso.
4. Stir to combine all Ingredients.

Nutrition information:
Calories: 242. Fat: 9.6 g. Cholesterol: 13 mg. Sodium: 220 mg. Carbohydrates: 31 g. Protein: 10 g.

45. Gingerbread Latte

Gingerbread Latte is a delightful and cozy beverage that combines the warm flavors of gingerbread with the rich and creamy taste of a latte. This festive drink is perfect for the holiday season or any time you want to treat yourself to a special coffee treat. With a hint of spice and a touch of sweetness, this Gingerbread Latte is sure to become a favorite.
Serving: 1
Preparation time: 5 minutes

Ready time: 10 minutes

Ingredients:
- 1 cup of milk
- 1 tablespoon of molasses
- 1 tablespoon of brown sugar
- 1/2 teaspoon of ground ginger
- 1/4 teaspoon of ground cinnamon
- 1/4 teaspoon of ground nutmeg
- 1/4 teaspoon of vanilla extract
- 1 shot of espresso or 1/2 cup of strong brewed coffee
- Whipped cream (optional)
- Ground cinnamon or nutmeg for garnish (optional)

Instructions:
1. In a small saucepan, heat the milk over medium heat until hot but not boiling. Stir occasionally to prevent scorching.
2. In a separate bowl, whisk together the molasses, brown sugar, ground ginger, ground cinnamon, ground nutmeg, and vanilla extract until well combined.
3. Pour the molasses mixture into the hot milk and whisk until fully incorporated.
4. If using an espresso machine, prepare a shot of espresso. If using brewed coffee, make sure it is strong and hot.
5. Pour the espresso or brewed coffee into a mug.
6. Slowly pour the gingerbread milk mixture over the espresso or coffee, stirring gently to combine.
7. If desired, top with whipped cream and sprinkle with ground cinnamon or nutmeg for garnish.
8. Serve hot and enjoy!

Nutrition information:
- Calories: 180
- Fat: 4g
- Carbohydrates: 30g
- Protein: 8g
- Sugar: 25g
- Fiber: 1g
- Sodium: 100mg

Note: Nutrition information may vary depending on the type of milk and sweetener used.

46. Maple Pecan Latte

Indulge in the cozy flavors of fall with this delightful Maple Pecan Latte. This warm and comforting beverage combines the rich taste of maple syrup with the nutty goodness of pecans, creating a perfect treat for those chilly mornings or relaxing evenings. With just a few simple Ingredients and easy steps, you can enjoy this delicious latte in the comfort of your own home.

Serving: 1
Preparation time: 5 minutes
Ready time: 10 minutes

Ingredients:
- 1 cup of milk
- 1 shot of espresso or 1/2 cup of strong brewed coffee
- 2 tablespoons of maple syrup
- 1 tablespoon of chopped pecans
- Whipped cream (optional)
- Ground cinnamon (optional)

Instructions:
1. In a small saucepan, heat the milk over medium heat until hot but not boiling.
2. While the milk is heating, brew a shot of espresso or prepare 1/2 cup of strong brewed coffee.
3. In a mug, combine the hot milk, espresso or coffee, maple syrup, and chopped pecans. Stir well to combine.
4. If desired, top the latte with whipped cream and a sprinkle of ground cinnamon.
5. Serve immediately and enjoy the comforting flavors of the Maple Pecan Latte.

Nutrition information:
- Calories: 180
- Fat: 7g

- Carbohydrates: 23g
- Protein: 8g
- Sugar: 19g
- Fiber: 1g
- Sodium: 100mg

Note: Nutrition information may vary depending on the type and quantity of Ingredients used.

47. Cardamom Spiced Latte

Cardamom Spiced Latte is a delightful and aromatic beverage that combines the rich flavors of coffee with the warm and exotic notes of cardamom. This comforting drink is perfect for cozy mornings or as an afternoon pick-me-up. With just a few simple Ingredients, you can create a delicious latte that will awaken your senses and leave you feeling satisfied.

Serving: 1
Preparation time: 5 minutes
Ready time: 10 minutes

Ingredients:
- 1 cup of milk (any type - dairy or plant-based)
- 1 tablespoon of ground coffee
- 1/4 teaspoon of ground cardamom
- 1 tablespoon of honey or sweetener of your choice
- A pinch of ground cinnamon (optional)
- Whipped cream (optional, for serving)
- Ground cardamom (for garnish)

Instructions:
1. In a small saucepan, heat the milk over medium heat until it starts to steam. Do not let it boil.
2. While the milk is heating, in a separate mug, combine the ground coffee and ground cardamom.
3. Pour the hot milk over the coffee and cardamom mixture, stirring well to combine.
4. Let the mixture steep for about 5 minutes to infuse the flavors.

5. After steeping, strain the latte into a clean mug to remove any coffee grounds or cardamom residue.
6. Stir in the honey or sweetener of your choice until it is fully dissolved.
7. If desired, sprinkle a pinch of ground cinnamon on top for an extra touch of warmth and flavor.
8. Optional: Top with whipped cream and a sprinkle of ground cardamom for an indulgent treat.
9. Serve the Cardamom Spiced Latte hot and enjoy!

Nutrition information:
- Calories: 120
- Fat: 4g
- Carbohydrates: 15g
- Protein: 6g
- Fiber: 1g
- Sugar: 14g
- Sodium: 100mg

Note: Nutrition information may vary depending on the type of milk and sweetener used.

48. Lavender Honey Latte

Lavender Honey Latte is a delightful and soothing beverage that combines the floral notes of lavender with the sweetness of honey. This latte is perfect for those looking for a unique and comforting drink to enjoy any time of the day. With just a few simple Ingredients, you can create a delicious lavender-infused latte that will warm your soul.
Serving: 1 Serving: Preparation time: 5 minutes
Ready time: 10 minutes

Ingredients:
- 1 cup of milk (any type of milk you prefer)
- 1 tablespoon dried culinary lavender
- 1 tablespoon honey
- 1 shot of espresso or 1/2 cup of strong brewed coffee
- Optional: whipped cream and additional dried lavender for garnish

Instructions:

1. In a small saucepan, heat the milk over medium-low heat until it starts to steam. Be careful not to let it boil.
2. Once the milk is steaming, add the dried lavender to the saucepan and let it steep for about 5 minutes. Stir occasionally to infuse the lavender flavor into the milk.
3. While the milk is steeping, prepare your espresso or strong brewed coffee.
4. After 5 minutes, strain the milk to remove the dried lavender. You can use a fine-mesh strainer or cheesecloth for this step.
5. Return the infused milk to the saucepan and add the honey. Stir well until the honey is fully dissolved.
6. Froth the milk using a milk frother or by vigorously whisking it until it becomes creamy and frothy.
7. Pour the espresso or brewed coffee into a mug, then slowly pour the frothed lavender honey milk over it.
8. Optional: Top with whipped cream and sprinkle some dried lavender on top for an extra touch of elegance.
9. Serve immediately and enjoy your homemade Lavender Honey Latte!

Nutrition information:
- Calories: 150
- Fat: 4g
- Carbohydrates: 22g
- Protein: 8g
- Sugar: 20g
- Fiber: 0g
- Sodium: 100mg

Note: Nutrition information may vary depending on the type of milk and honey used.

49. Raspberry Mocha

Raspberry Mocha is an indulgent coffee-based smoothie perfect for a sweet morning or after-dinner caffeine fix. This sweet and creamy blend is made with espresso, milk, fresh raspberries, and sweetener, and blended until smooth for the ultimate treat.
Serving: 4
Preparation time: 10 minutes

Ready time: 10 minutes

Ingredients:
- 2 shots of espresso
- 2 cups whole milk
- 1 cup fresh raspberries
- 2 tablespoons honey
- 3 tablespoons cocoa powder

Instructions:
1. Begin by brewing two shots of espresso.
2. In a blender or food processor, combine the brewed espresso, whole milk, fresh raspberries, honey, and cocoa powder. Blend until completely smooth.
3. Divide the raspberry mocha evenly between four glasses.
4. Serve immediately.

Nutrition information:
Serving size 4, 280 Kcal, Fat 10.6g, Carbs 37.3g, Protein 9.7g, Cholesterol 33mg, Sodium 134mg, Sugar 31.2g

50. Nutella Latte

Indulge in the perfect combination of rich Nutella and creamy latte with this delightful Nutella Latte recipe. This comforting beverage is a treat for all coffee and chocolate lovers, providing a delicious and satisfying drink to enjoy any time of the day.
Serving: 1 Serving: Preparation time: 5 minutes
Ready time: 10 minutes

Ingredients:
- 1 cup of milk
- 1 tablespoon of Nutella
- 1 shot of espresso or 1/2 cup of strong brewed coffee
- Whipped cream (optional)
- Cocoa powder or chocolate shavings for garnish (optional)

Instructions:

1. In a small saucepan, heat the milk over medium heat until it starts to steam. Do not let it boil.
2. Add the Nutella to the saucepan and whisk until it is fully melted and incorporated into the milk.
3. If using espresso, brew a shot of espresso. If using coffee, make sure it is strong and hot.
4. Pour the espresso or coffee into a mug.
5. Slowly pour the Nutella milk mixture into the mug, stirring gently to combine.
6. If desired, top with whipped cream and sprinkle with cocoa powder or chocolate shavings for an extra touch of indulgence.
7. Serve hot and enjoy!

Nutrition information per Serving: - Calories: 200
- Fat: 8g
- Carbohydrates: 25g
- Protein: 8g
- Sugar: 22g
- Fiber: 1g

Note: Nutrition information may vary depending on the type and brand of Ingredients used.

51. Cinnamon Dolce Latte

Cinnamon Dolce Latte is a delicious and comforting coffee beverage that combines the rich flavors of cinnamon and espresso with creamy milk. This warm and aromatic drink is perfect for cozy mornings or as an afternoon pick-me-up. With just a few simple Ingredients, you can easily recreate this popular Starbucks drink at home.

Serving: 1
Preparation time: 5 minutes
Ready time: 10 minutes

Ingredients:
- 1 cup of milk
- 1 shot of espresso (or 1/2 cup of strong brewed coffee)
- 1 tablespoon of cinnamon syrup
- Whipped cream (optional)

- Ground cinnamon for garnish

Instructions:
1. In a small saucepan, heat the milk over medium heat until hot but not boiling.
2. While the milk is heating, brew a shot of espresso or prepare 1/2 cup of strong brewed coffee.
3. Once the milk is hot, remove it from the heat and whisk vigorously until frothy.
4. In a large mug, combine the frothy milk, espresso (or coffee), and cinnamon syrup. Stir well to combine.
5. If desired, top the latte with a dollop of whipped cream and sprinkle with ground cinnamon for garnish.
6. Serve hot and enjoy!

Nutrition information:
- Calories: 150
- Fat: 5g
- Carbohydrates: 20g
- Protein: 8g
- Sugar: 18g
- Fiber: 1g

Note: Nutrition information may vary depending on the specific brands and quantities of Ingredients used.

52. Salted Caramel Latte

Try this delicious salted caramel latte for a single serving – it's the perfect pick-me-up treat!
Serving: Single-Serving: Preparation time: 5 minutes
Ready time: 5 minutes

Ingredients:
- 1 shot of espresso
- 4 tsp granulated sugar
- 2 tsp caramel sauce
- ½ tsp sea salt
- ¾ cup hot milk

Instructions:

1. Combine the espresso, sugar, caramel sauce and sea salt in a cup. Stir until the sugar and salt are dissolved.
2. Pour in the hot milk and stir.
3. Garnish with a sprinkle of sea salt and caramel sauce, if desired.

Nutrition information:

Calories: 127 kcal, Carbohydrates: 18.6 g, Protein: 4.2 g, Fat: 3.3 g, Saturated Fat: 1.8 g, Cholesterol: 9 mg, Sodium: 220 mg, Potassium: 131 mg, Sugar: 17.2 g, Vitamin A: 140 IU, Calcium: 157 mg.

53. Caramel Brulee Latte

Indulge in the rich and creamy goodness of a Caramel Brulee Latte. This delightful beverage combines the smoothness of caramel with the boldness of coffee, creating a perfect treat for any time of the day. Whether you're a coffee lover or simply looking for a sweet pick-me-up, this recipe will surely satisfy your cravings.

Serving: 1 cup
Preparation time: 5 minutes
Ready time: 10 minutes

Ingredients:

- 1 cup of milk
- 1 shot of espresso or 1/2 cup of strong brewed coffee
- 2 tablespoons of caramel sauce
- 1 tablespoon of brown sugar
- 1/2 teaspoon of vanilla extract
- Whipped cream (optional)
- Caramel drizzle (optional)

Instructions:

1. In a small saucepan, heat the milk over medium heat until it starts to steam. Do not let it boil.
2. While the milk is heating, brew a shot of espresso or prepare 1/2 cup of strong coffee.

3. In a separate microwave-safe bowl, combine the caramel sauce, brown sugar, and vanilla extract. Microwave for 30 seconds or until the mixture becomes smooth and well combined.
4. Pour the hot milk into a blender and add the caramel mixture. Blend on high speed for about 30 seconds until frothy.
5. Pour the espresso or coffee into a mug, then slowly pour the frothy milk mixture over it.
6. If desired, top with whipped cream and drizzle some caramel sauce on top for an extra touch of sweetness.
7. Serve immediately and enjoy!

Nutrition information:
- Calories: 180
- Fat: 5g
- Carbohydrates: 30g
- Protein: 6g
- Sugar: 25g
- Sodium: 100mg

Note: Nutrition information may vary depending on the specific brands and quantities of Ingredients used.

54. Tiramisu Latte

Tiramisu Latte is a heavenly twist on a traditional coffee classic. With a delectable blend of espresso and whipped cream flavored with cocoa powder and a touch of rum essence, this is the perfect coffee for those looking for a unique treat.

Serving: 2
Preparation time: 5 minutes
Ready time: 15 minutes

Ingredients:
- 2 cups of espresso
- 1 cup of cream
- 2 tbsp cocoa powder
- 2 tsp of rum essence

Instructions:

1. Brew two cups of espresso and set aside.
2. In a medium bowl, whip together the cream, cocoa powder, and rum essence into a thick creamy texture.
3. Divide the espresso between two mugs and top with the whipped cream mixture.
4. Sprinkle with cocoa powder and/or chopped espresso beans before serving.

Nutrition information: Per serving, calories 157, fat 9 g, saturated fat 5 g, cholesterol 27 mg, sodium 23 mg, carbohydrate 9 g, fiber 1 g, sugars 0 g, protein 3 g.

55. Coconut Caramel Latte

Indulge in the creamy and aromatic delight of a Coconut Caramel Latte. This heavenly beverage combines the rich flavors of coconut, caramel, and espresso to create a comforting and satisfying treat. Whether you enjoy it as a morning pick-me-up or a cozy afternoon indulgence, this latte is sure to become your new favorite.
Serving: 1 Serving: Preparation time: 5 minutes
Ready time: 10 minutes

Ingredients:
- 1 shot of espresso (or 1/2 cup of strong brewed coffee)
- 1 cup of milk (dairy or plant-based)
- 2 tablespoons of coconut syrup
- 1 tablespoon of caramel sauce
- Whipped cream (optional)
- Shredded coconut (optional, for garnish)

Instructions:
1. Brew a shot of espresso using your espresso machine or prepare 1/2 cup of strong brewed coffee.
2. In a small saucepan, heat the milk over medium heat until hot but not boiling. Alternatively, you can heat the milk in the microwave for about 1-2 minutes.
3. In a mug, combine the hot espresso, coconut syrup, and caramel sauce. Stir well to combine.

4. Pour the hot milk into the mug, slowly and carefully, to create a creamy latte. Stir gently to incorporate all the flavors.
5. If desired, top the latte with whipped cream and sprinkle some shredded coconut on top for an extra touch of indulgence.
6. Serve the Coconut Caramel Latte immediately and enjoy its warm and comforting flavors.

Nutrition information:
- Calories: 180
- Fat: 6g
- Carbohydrates: 25g
- Protein: 8g
- Sugar: 20g
- Fiber: 0g
- Sodium: 100mg

Note: Nutrition information may vary depending on the specific brands and quantities of Ingredients used.

56. Pistachio Mocha

Indulge in the rich and nutty flavors of our Pistachio Mocha. This delightful beverage combines the smoothness of mocha with the irresistible taste of pistachios. Perfect for a cozy afternoon treat or a pick-me-up in the morning, this recipe will surely satisfy your cravings.
Serving: 1 Serving: Preparation time: 5 minutes
Ready time: 10 minutes

Ingredients:
- 1 cup of milk
- 1 shot of espresso (or 1/2 cup of strong brewed coffee)
- 2 tablespoons of pistachio syrup
- 1 tablespoon of cocoa powder
- Whipped cream, for topping
- Crushed pistachios, for garnish

Instructions:
1. In a small saucepan, heat the milk over medium heat until hot but not boiling.

2. In a mug, combine the espresso (or coffee), pistachio syrup, and cocoa powder. Stir until well mixed.
3. Pour the hot milk into the mug and stir gently to combine all the Ingredients.
4. Top with a dollop of whipped cream and sprinkle with crushed pistachios.
5. Serve immediately and enjoy the delightful flavors of the Pistachio Mocha.

Nutrition information:
- Calories: 180
- Fat: 8g
- Carbohydrates: 20g
- Protein: 8g
- Fiber: 2g
- Sugar: 16g
- Sodium: 100mg

Note: Nutrition information may vary depending on the specific brands and quantities of Ingredients used.

57. Chocolate Mint Latte

Indulge in the rich and refreshing flavors of our Chocolate Mint Latte. This delightful beverage combines the smoothness of chocolate with the invigorating taste of mint, creating a perfect treat for any time of the day. Whether you're a coffee lover or simply enjoy a cozy drink, this recipe is sure to satisfy your cravings.

Serving: 1 cup
Preparation time: 5 minutes
Ready time: 10 minutes

Ingredients:
- 1 cup milk
- 1 tablespoon cocoa powder
- 1 tablespoon sugar
- 1/4 teaspoon peppermint extract
- 1/4 cup brewed coffee or espresso
- Whipped cream (optional)

- Chocolate shavings (optional)

Instructions:
1. In a small saucepan, heat the milk over medium heat until it starts to steam. Do not let it boil.
2. In a separate bowl, whisk together the cocoa powder and sugar until well combined.
3. Slowly add the cocoa powder mixture to the steaming milk, whisking constantly to prevent any lumps from forming.
4. Stir in the peppermint extract and continue to heat the mixture until it reaches your desired temperature.
5. Meanwhile, brew a fresh cup of coffee or espresso.
6. Once the milk mixture is heated, remove it from the heat and pour it into a mug.
7. Add the brewed coffee or espresso to the mug and stir well to combine.
8. If desired, top the latte with whipped cream and sprinkle with chocolate shavings for an extra touch of indulgence.
9. Serve hot and enjoy!

Nutrition information:
- Calories: 150
- Fat: 4g
- Carbohydrates: 22g
- Protein: 8g
- Fiber: 2g
- Sugar: 18g
- Sodium: 100mg

Note: Nutrition information may vary depending on the specific brands and quantities of Ingredients used.

58. Caramelized Banana Latte

Indulge in the rich and creamy flavors of our Caramelized Banana Latte. This delightful beverage combines the sweetness of caramelized bananas with the smoothness of a latte, creating a perfect treat for any time of the day. Whether you're a coffee lover or simply enjoy a comforting drink, this recipe is sure to satisfy your cravings.

Serving: 1 Serving: Preparation time: 5 minutes
Ready time: 10 minutes

Ingredients:
- 1 ripe banana
- 1 tablespoon brown sugar
- 1 cup milk
- 1 shot of espresso or 1/2 cup strong brewed coffee
- 1/2 teaspoon vanilla extract
- Whipped cream (optional)
- Caramel sauce (optional)

Instructions:
1. Start by caramelizing the banana. Peel the banana and slice it into thin rounds.
2. In a non-stick skillet, sprinkle the brown sugar evenly and heat over medium heat until it starts to melt.
3. Add the banana slices to the skillet and cook for about 2-3 minutes on each side, until they turn golden brown and caramelized. Remove from heat and set aside.
4. In a small saucepan, heat the milk over medium-low heat until hot but not boiling. Remove from heat and whisk vigorously until frothy.
5. Brew a shot of espresso or make a strong cup of coffee.
6. In a large mug, combine the caramelized banana slices, espresso or coffee, and vanilla extract.
7. Pour the frothy milk over the banana and coffee mixture, stirring gently to combine.
8. If desired, top with whipped cream and drizzle with caramel sauce for an extra touch of indulgence.
9. Serve hot and enjoy!

Nutrition information:
- Calories: 180
- Fat: 4g
- Carbohydrates: 32g
- Protein: 6g
- Sugar: 22g
- Fiber: 2g
- Sodium: 80mg

Note: Nutrition information may vary depending on the specific Ingredients and brands used.

59. Matcha Green Tea Latte

This Matcha Green Tea Latte is the perfect way to enjoy the delicious taste and amazing health benefits of matcha green tea in a creamy and delicious drink.
Serving: Makes one Matcha Green Tea Latte
Preparation Time: 5 minutes
Ready Time: 5 minutes

Ingredients:
-1 teaspoon matcha green tea powder
-2 teaspoons of hot water
-3/4 cup of steamed or warm milk
-Optional: 1 teaspoon of honey or sugar

Instructions:
1. Combine the matcha green tea powder and the hot water in a mug.
2. Mix until there are no more lumps in the liquid, then add steamed or warm milk.
3. Using a hand mixer or frother, blend the mixture together until creamy and top with a sprinkle of matcha green tea powder.
4. Optionally, add 1 teaspoon of honey or sugar for sweetness.

Nutrition information: Per Serving- Calories: 73, Carbohydrates: 6.4g, Protein: 2.4g, Sodium: 24mg, Fat: 2.2g, Sugar: 5.4

60. Golden Milk Latte

Golden Milk Latte is a delicious and healthy beverage that has gained popularity for its numerous health benefits. This warm and comforting drink is made with a combination of turmeric, ginger, cinnamon, and other spices, which not only give it a vibrant golden color but also provide a range of antioxidants and anti-inflammatory properties.

Whether you enjoy it in the morning as a pick-me-up or in the evening to unwind, this Golden Milk Latte is sure to become a favorite.

Serving: 1
Preparation time: 5 minutes
Ready time: 10 minutes

Ingredients:
- 1 cup of milk (dairy or plant-based)
- 1 teaspoon of ground turmeric
- 1/2 teaspoon of ground ginger
- 1/2 teaspoon of ground cinnamon
- 1/4 teaspoon of ground cardamom
- 1/4 teaspoon of vanilla extract
- 1 tablespoon of honey or maple syrup (adjust to taste)
- A pinch of black pepper (optional)

Instructions:
1. In a small saucepan, heat the milk over medium heat until it starts to steam. Be careful not to let it boil.
2. Add the turmeric, ginger, cinnamon, cardamom, and vanilla extract to the saucepan. Whisk well to combine the spices with the milk.
3. Continue to heat the mixture for another 5 minutes, stirring occasionally to prevent it from sticking to the bottom of the pan.
4. Remove the saucepan from the heat and let the mixture cool for a minute.
5. Stir in the honey or maple syrup, adjusting the sweetness to your liking.
6. If desired, add a pinch of black pepper to enhance the absorption of turmeric's beneficial properties.
7. Pour the Golden Milk Latte into a mug and serve warm.

Nutrition information:
- Calories: 150
- Fat: 5g
- Carbohydrates: 20g
- Protein: 8g
- Fiber: 2g
- Sugar: 15g
- Sodium: 100mg

Note: Nutrition information may vary depending on the type of milk and sweetener used.

61. Irish Cream Latte

Irish Cream Latte is a delightful and creamy coffee beverage that combines the rich flavors of Irish cream liqueur with a smooth espresso shot. This indulgent drink is perfect for those cozy mornings or as an after-dinner treat. With just a few simple Ingredients, you can easily recreate this delicious drink at home and enjoy the comforting flavors of Ireland.
Serving: 1 Serving: Preparation time: 5 minutes
Ready time: 5 minutes

Ingredients:
- 1 shot of espresso
- 1/2 cup of milk
- 1 tablespoon of Irish cream liqueur
- 1 teaspoon of sugar (optional)
- Whipped cream (for garnish)
- Cocoa powder or cinnamon (for garnish)

Instructions:
1. Brew a shot of espresso using your preferred method. Set it aside.
2. In a small saucepan, heat the milk over medium heat until it starts to steam. Do not let it boil.
3. Once the milk is steaming, remove it from the heat and whisk vigorously until it becomes frothy.
4. Pour the hot espresso shot into a mug.
5. Add the Irish cream liqueur to the mug and stir gently to combine.
6. Slowly pour the frothy milk into the mug, holding back the foam with a spoon to create a layered effect.
7. If desired, add sugar to taste and stir until dissolved.
8. Top the latte with a dollop of whipped cream.
9. Sprinkle cocoa powder or cinnamon on top for an extra touch of flavor and presentation.
10. Serve immediately and enjoy the creamy and indulgent Irish Cream Latte.

Nutrition information:
- Calories: 150
- Fat: 6g
- Carbohydrates: 12g
- Protein: 5g
- Sugar: 10g
- Fiber: 0g
- Sodium: 60mg

Note: Nutrition information may vary depending on the specific brands and quantities of Ingredients used.

62. Raspberry White Mocha

Start your day with the perfect drink, a Raspberry White Mocha. This delicious combination of white chocolate, raspberries, and espresso will make for a tantalizing beverage.

Serving: 1
Preparation Time: 5 minutes
Ready Time: 5 minutes

Ingredients:
- ¼ cup of white chocolate chips
- 2 shots of espresso
- 2 tablespoons of raspberry syrup
- 1 cup of milk

Instructions:
1. Start by heating the milk for about 2 minutes so that it forms a light foam.
2. While the milk is heating up, add the white chocolate chips and raspberry syrup into a glass and stir.
3. Once the milk is heated, pour it into the glass with the syrup and chocolate.
4. Add 2 shots of espresso and give the mixture a good stir.
5. Let the Raspberry White Mocha cool for a few minutes and then enjoy!

Nutrition information:
Calories: 262 kcal, Carbohydrates: 23 g, Protein: 8 g, Fat: 13g, Sodium: 77 mg, Sugar: 13 g.

63. Pumpkin Caramel Latte

Pumpkin Caramel Latte is a delicious treat for the fall season packed with warming and flavorful Ingredients. Enjoy this classic drink with a smile and savor its comforting sweetness.
Serving: 1
Preparation time: 5 minutes
Ready time: 15 minutes

Ingredients:
- 1 cup of freshly brewed espresso
- 2 tablespoons of pumpkin puree
- 1/4 cup of caramel syrup
- 2 cups of milk
- Whipped cream (optional)

Instructions:
1. In a small saucepan, heat the milk over medium-low heat, until hot throughout.
2. Pour espresso and pumpkin puree into a blender and blend until frothy.
3. Add the hot milk to the espresso and pumpkin puree mixture and blend until combined.
4. Pour the blended mixture into a mug and add in the caramel syrup.
5. Top with whipped cream and a sprinkle of cinnamon (optional).

Nutrition information: Calories: 250, Fat: 7g, Carbohydrates: 37g, Sugar: 24g, Protein: 10g

64. Hazelnut White Mocha

Treat yourself to a decadent and delicious Hazelnut White Mocha. Made with rich espresso and creamy white chocolate, this delicious coffee

beverage is perfect for a special occasion or simply to enjoy on a cozy day in.
Serving: 1
Preparation time: 4 minutes
Ready time: 4 minutes

Ingredients:
- ½ cup ground espresso
- 2 tablespoons white chocolate chips
- 2 teaspoons hazelnut flavored syrup
- 2 tablespoons half and half cream
- Hot Water
- Whipped cream (optional)

Instructions:
1. Put the espresso and white chocolate chips in a mug or French press.
2. Pour hot water over the espresso and white chocolate chips and stir until fully combined.
3. Add the hazelnut flavored syrup and cream.
4. Stir until all Ingredients are fully mixed.
5. For the finishing touch, top your coffee with some whipped cream for a special treat.

Nutrition information:
Calories: 90, Total Fat: 4g, Saturated Fat: 2.5g, Trans Fat: 0g, Cholesterol: 5mg, Sodium: 15mg, Carbohydrates: 13g, Fiber: 1g, Sugar: 9g, Protein: 1g.

65. Almond Joy Latte

Indulge in the rich and creamy goodness of an Almond Joy Latte. This delightful beverage combines the flavors of chocolate, coconut, and almond to create a decadent treat that will satisfy your cravings. Whether you enjoy it as a morning pick-me-up or a cozy evening drink, this Almond Joy Latte is sure to become your new favorite.
Serving: 1
Preparation time: 5 minutes
Ready time: 10 minutes

Ingredients:
- 1 cup of strong brewed coffee
- 1 cup of milk (any type you prefer)
- 2 tablespoons of chocolate syrup
- 1 tablespoon of coconut syrup
- 1 tablespoon of almond syrup
- Whipped cream (optional)
- Shredded coconut (optional)
- Almond slices (optional)

Instructions:
1. Brew a cup of strong coffee using your preferred method. Set it aside.
2. In a small saucepan, heat the milk over medium heat until it starts to steam. Do not let it boil.
3. In a coffee mug, combine the chocolate syrup, coconut syrup, and almond syrup.
4. Pour the hot coffee into the mug and stir well to combine the syrups.
5. Slowly pour the steamed milk into the mug, stirring gently to mix everything together.
6. If desired, top the latte with whipped cream, shredded coconut, and almond slices for an extra touch of indulgence.
7. Serve the Almond Joy Latte hot and enjoy!

Nutrition information:
- Calories: 200
- Fat: 6g
- Carbohydrates: 30g
- Protein: 8g
- Sugar: 20g
- Fiber: 2g

Note: Nutrition information may vary depending on the specific brands and quantities of Ingredients used.

66. Snickerdoodle Latte

The Snickerdoodle Latte is a delightful and cozy beverage that combines the flavors of a classic snickerdoodle cookie with a creamy latte. This comforting drink is perfect for chilly mornings or as an indulgent treat any time of the day. With its warm cinnamon and vanilla notes, it's sure to become a favorite for coffee lovers and cookie enthusiasts alike.

Serving: 1 Serving: Preparation time: 5 minutes

Ready time: 10 minutes

Ingredients:
- 1 cup of milk (any type you prefer, such as whole milk, almond milk, or oat milk)
- 1 shot of espresso or 1/2 cup of strong brewed coffee
- 1 tablespoon of granulated sugar
- 1/2 teaspoon of ground cinnamon
- 1/4 teaspoon of vanilla extract
- Whipped cream (optional)
- Ground cinnamon for garnish

Instructions:
1. In a small saucepan, heat the milk over medium heat until hot but not boiling. Stir occasionally to prevent scorching.
2. While the milk is heating, brew a shot of espresso or make a strong cup of coffee.
3. In a separate small bowl, combine the granulated sugar and ground cinnamon.
4. Once the milk is hot, remove it from the heat and whisk in the vanilla extract.
5. Pour the hot milk into a blender or use a frother to create a creamy foam.
6. In a large mug, combine the brewed espresso or coffee with the cinnamon-sugar mixture. Stir until the sugar has dissolved.
7. Slowly pour the frothed milk over the coffee mixture, holding back the foam with a spoon to create a layered effect.
8. Top with whipped cream, if desired, and sprinkle with a pinch of ground cinnamon for garnish.
9. Serve immediately and enjoy the comforting flavors of a Snickerdoodle Latte.

Nutrition information:
- Calories: 150
- Fat: 5g
- Carbohydrates: 20g

- Protein: 8g
- Sugar: 15g
- Fiber: 1g
- Sodium: 100mg

Note: Nutrition information may vary depending on the type of milk and additional toppings used.

67. Maple Cinnamon Latte

Indulge in the cozy flavors of fall with this delicious Maple Cinnamon Latte. Made with a perfect blend of rich espresso, sweet maple syrup, and warm cinnamon, this latte is the ultimate comfort drink. Whether you're starting your day or looking for a pick-me-up in the afternoon, this latte is sure to satisfy your cravings and warm your soul.

Serving: 1 Serving: Preparation time: 5 minutes
Ready time: 10 minutes

Ingredients:
- 1 shot of espresso (or 1/2 cup of strong brewed coffee)
- 1 cup of milk (any type you prefer)
- 2 tablespoons of pure maple syrup
- 1/4 teaspoon of ground cinnamon
- Whipped cream (optional, for topping)
- Ground cinnamon (optional, for garnish)

Instructions:
1. Brew a shot of espresso using your espresso machine or make a strong cup of coffee using your preferred method.
2. In a small saucepan, heat the milk over medium-low heat until hot but not boiling. You can also heat the milk in the microwave for about 1-2 minutes.
3. In a mug, combine the hot espresso, maple syrup, and ground cinnamon. Stir well to combine.
4. Pour the hot milk into the mug, holding back the foam with a spoon. Stir gently to mix the flavors.
5. If desired, top the latte with whipped cream and sprinkle some ground cinnamon on top for an extra touch of indulgence.
6. Serve the Maple Cinnamon Latte hot and enjoy!

Nutrition information:
- Calories: 150
- Fat: 4g
- Carbohydrates: 24g
- Protein: 6g
- Sugar: 20g
- Fiber: 0g
- Sodium: 100mg

Note: Nutrition information may vary depending on the type of milk and maple syrup used.

68. Pistachio White Mocha

Indulge in the rich and creamy flavors of our Pistachio White Mocha. This delightful beverage combines the nutty essence of pistachios with the smoothness of white chocolate, creating a heavenly treat for your taste buds. Whether you're looking for a cozy drink to enjoy on a chilly day or a special treat to satisfy your sweet tooth, this Pistachio White Mocha is sure to become a favorite.

Serving: 1
Preparation time: 5 minutes
Ready time: 10 minutes

Ingredients:
- 1 shot of espresso or 1/2 cup of strong brewed coffee
- 1 cup of milk
- 2 tablespoons of white chocolate chips
- 1 tablespoon of pistachio syrup
- Whipped cream (optional)
- Crushed pistachios (optional)

Instructions:
1. In a small saucepan, heat the milk over medium heat until hot but not boiling. Stir occasionally to prevent scorching.
2. In a microwave-safe bowl, melt the white chocolate chips in the microwave for 30-second intervals, stirring in between, until fully melted and smooth.

3. Add the melted white chocolate to the hot milk, stirring until well combined.
4. Brew a shot of espresso or prepare 1/2 cup of strong brewed coffee.
5. Pour the espresso or coffee into a mug.
6. Add the pistachio syrup to the mug and stir to combine.
7. Slowly pour the hot milk and white chocolate mixture into the mug, stirring gently to incorporate all the flavors.
8. If desired, top with whipped cream and a sprinkle of crushed pistachios for an extra touch of indulgence.
9. Serve hot and enjoy!

Nutrition information:
- Calories: 250
- Fat: 12g
- Carbohydrates: 28g
- Protein: 8g
- Sugar: 24g
- Fiber: 1g
- Sodium: 100mg

Note: Nutrition information may vary depending on the specific brands and quantities of Ingredients used.

69. Nutella Mocha

Indulge in the perfect blend of rich chocolate and smooth coffee with our delectable Nutella Mocha recipe. This delightful beverage is a heavenly combination of creamy Nutella and bold espresso, creating a drink that will satisfy your sweet tooth and give you a much-needed caffeine boost. Whether you enjoy it as a morning pick-me-up or a cozy treat on a chilly evening, the Nutella Mocha is sure to become your new favorite indulgence.

Serving: 1
Preparation time: 5 minutes
Ready time: 5 minutes

Ingredients:
- 1 cup milk
- 1 shot of espresso (or 1/2 cup strong brewed coffee)

- 2 tablespoons Nutella
- Whipped cream (optional)
- Cocoa powder (for garnish)

Instructions:

1. In a small saucepan, heat the milk over medium heat until hot but not boiling.
2. In a separate cup, prepare your espresso or strong brewed coffee.
3. In a microwave-safe bowl, melt the Nutella for about 20 seconds until it becomes smooth and pourable.
4. Pour the hot milk into a blender or use a handheld frother to froth the milk until it becomes creamy and frothy.
5. In a large mug, add the melted Nutella and the prepared espresso or coffee.
6. Slowly pour the frothed milk into the mug, stirring gently to combine all the Ingredients.
7. If desired, top with a dollop of whipped cream and sprinkle with cocoa powder for an extra touch of decadence.
8. Serve immediately and enjoy the rich and velvety Nutella Mocha!

Nutrition information:
- Calories: 250
- Fat: 12g
- Carbohydrates: 28g
- Protein: 8g
- Sugar: 24g
- Fiber: 2g
- Sodium: 100mg

Note: Nutrition information may vary depending on the specific brands and quantities of Ingredients used.

70. Spiced Apple Latte

Spiced Apple Latte is a delightful and comforting beverage that combines the flavors of warm spices and sweet apples with the richness of a latte. This cozy drink is perfect for chilly mornings or as an afternoon pick-me-up. With just a few simple Ingredients, you can create a delicious spiced apple latte right in the comfort of your own home.

Serving: 1 Serving: Preparation time: 5 minutes
Ready time: 10 minutes

Ingredients:
- 1 cup of milk (dairy or plant-based)
- 1/2 cup of apple juice
- 1 tablespoon of brown sugar
- 1/2 teaspoon of ground cinnamon
- 1/4 teaspoon of ground nutmeg
- 1/4 teaspoon of ground cloves
- 1/4 teaspoon of vanilla extract
- 1 shot of espresso or 1/2 cup of strong brewed coffee
- Whipped cream (optional)
- Cinnamon stick (optional, for garnish)

Instructions:
1. In a small saucepan, heat the milk and apple juice over medium heat until hot but not boiling. Stir occasionally to prevent scorching.
2. Add the brown sugar, ground cinnamon, ground nutmeg, ground cloves, and vanilla extract to the saucepan. Whisk until the sugar is dissolved and the spices are well combined.
3. If using an espresso machine, prepare a shot of espresso. If not, brew a strong cup of coffee using your preferred method.
4. Pour the espresso or coffee into a large mug.
5. Slowly pour the spiced milk mixture over the espresso or coffee, using a spoon to hold back the foam.
6. Stir gently to combine the flavors.
7. If desired, top with whipped cream and sprinkle with a pinch of ground cinnamon.
8. Garnish with a cinnamon stick, if desired.
9. Serve hot and enjoy!

Nutrition information:
- Calories: 150
- Fat: 4g
- Carbohydrates: 25g
- Protein: 5g
- Fiber: 1g
- Sugar: 20g
- Sodium: 80mg

- Calcium: 150mg
- Iron: 0.5mg

Note: Nutrition information may vary depending on the type of milk and apple juice used.

71. Rosemary Honey Latte

Indulge in the aromatic and comforting flavors of a Rosemary Honey Latte. This delightful beverage combines the earthy notes of rosemary with the sweetness of honey, creating a unique and satisfying drink. Perfect for cozy mornings or as an afternoon pick-me-up, this latte is sure to become a favorite.

Serving: 1 Serving: Preparation time: 5 minutes
Ready time: 10 minutes

Ingredients:
- 1 cup of milk (any type of milk you prefer)
- 1 sprig of fresh rosemary
- 1 tablespoon of honey
- 1 shot of espresso or 1/2 cup of strong brewed coffee
- Ground cinnamon (optional, for garnish)

Instructions:
1. In a small saucepan, heat the milk over medium-low heat until it starts to steam. Be careful not to let it boil.
2. While the milk is heating, gently bruise the rosemary sprig by rolling it between your hands. This will help release its flavors.
3. Add the bruised rosemary sprig to the saucepan with the milk and let it steep for about 5 minutes. This will infuse the milk with the aroma of rosemary.
4. After 5 minutes, remove the rosemary sprig from the milk and discard it.
5. In a mug, combine the honey and espresso or strong brewed coffee. Stir until the honey is dissolved.
6. Pour the infused milk into the mug, using a spoon to hold back the foam.
7. Stir gently to combine all the Ingredients.

8. If desired, sprinkle a pinch of ground cinnamon on top for an extra touch of flavor and aroma.
9. Your Rosemary Honey Latte is now ready to be enjoyed!

Nutrition information:
- Calories: 150
- Fat: 4g
- Carbohydrates: 22g
- Protein: 8g
- Sugar: 20g
- Fiber: 0g
- Sodium: 100mg

Note: Nutrition information may vary depending on the type of milk and honey used.

72. S'mores Latte

S'mores Latte is a delicious and indulgent drink that combines the flavors of a classic campfire treat with the rich and creamy taste of a latte. This comforting beverage is perfect for cozy evenings or as a special treat to start your day. With the perfect balance of chocolate, marshmallow, and coffee, this S'mores Latte is sure to become your new favorite drink.
Serving: 1 Serving: Preparation time: 5 minutes
Ready time: 10 minutes

Ingredients:
- 1 cup of milk
- 1 shot of espresso or 1/2 cup of strong brewed coffee
- 2 tablespoons of chocolate syrup
- 1 tablespoon of marshmallow fluff
- 1 graham cracker, crushed
- Whipped cream, for topping

Instructions:
1. In a small saucepan, heat the milk over medium heat until hot but not boiling.
2. In a coffee mug, combine the espresso or brewed coffee with the chocolate syrup.

3. Pour the hot milk into the mug and stir well to combine.
4. Spoon the marshmallow fluff on top of the latte and use a spoon to swirl it into the drink.
5. Sprinkle the crushed graham cracker over the marshmallow fluff.
6. Top with whipped cream and an extra sprinkle of crushed graham cracker.
7. Serve immediately and enjoy!

Nutrition information:
- Calories: 250
- Fat: 8g
- Carbohydrates: 38g
- Protein: 7g
- Sugar: 28g
- Fiber: 1g

Note: Nutrition information may vary depending on the specific brands and quantities of Ingredients used.

73. Cinnamon Roll Latte

Indulge in the comforting flavors of a Cinnamon Roll Latte, a delightful beverage that combines the warmth of cinnamon with the richness of coffee. This creamy and aromatic drink is the perfect way to start your day or enjoy as a cozy treat during chilly evenings. With just a few simple Ingredients, you can easily recreate this delicious latte at home.

Serving: 1 Serving: Preparation time: 5 minutes
Ready time: 10 minutes

Ingredients:
- 1 cup of milk
- 1 tablespoon of ground cinnamon
- 1 tablespoon of brown sugar
- 1/2 teaspoon of vanilla extract
- 1/4 cup of brewed coffee or espresso
- Whipped cream (optional)
- Ground cinnamon for garnish (optional)

Instructions:

1. In a small saucepan, heat the milk over medium heat until it starts to steam. Do not let it boil.
2. Add the ground cinnamon, brown sugar, and vanilla extract to the saucepan. Whisk well until the sugar has dissolved and the cinnamon is evenly distributed.
3. Continue to heat the milk mixture for another 2-3 minutes, stirring occasionally, until it is hot but not boiling.
4. Meanwhile, brew your coffee or espresso separately.
5. Once the milk mixture is hot, remove it from the heat and froth it using a handheld frother or by vigorously whisking it.
6. Pour the brewed coffee or espresso into a mug.
7. Slowly pour the frothed milk over the coffee, holding back the foam with a spoon to create a layered effect.
8. If desired, top the latte with whipped cream and sprinkle some ground cinnamon on top for garnish.
9. Serve the Cinnamon Roll Latte immediately and enjoy!

Nutrition information:
- Calories: 150
- Fat: 4g
- Carbohydrates: 22g
- Protein: 8g
- Sugar: 18g
- Fiber: 1g
- Sodium: 100mg

Note: Nutrition information may vary depending on the type of milk and coffee used.

74. Peanut Butter Cup Latte

Create a delicious and creamy peanut butter cup latte that is perfect for an indulgent breakfast or afternoon energising pick-me-up.
Serving: 1
Preparation time: 5 minutes
Ready time: 5 minutes

Ingredients:
- 2 shots of espresso

- 2 tbsp of peanut butter
- 2 tbsp of chocolate syrup
- 120ml of steamed milk
- 2 tbsp of whipped cream
- A sprinkle of chocolate flakes

Instructions:
1. Begin by brewing 2 shots of espresso and adding them to a mug.
2. Add the peanut butter and chocolate syrup to the mug and stir thoroughly.
3. Pour the steamed milk into the mug and stir again.
4. Top the mixture with whipped cream and chocolate flakes.

Nutrition information (per serving):
- Calories: 202 kcal
- Total Fat: 11.7g
- Saturated Fat: 5.2g
- Total Carbohydrate: 16.2g
- Protein: 8.2g

75. Strawberry Cheesecake Latte

This Strawberry Cheesecake Latte recipe is a delicious combination of creamy and fruity flavors. It's sure to satisfy your sweet tooth and make your afternoon coffee break extra special.
Serving: 1 cup
Preparation time: 5 minutes
Ready time: 5 minutes

Ingredients:
- 2 shots of espresso
- 2 tablespoons strawberry flavor syrup
- 2 tablespoons of cream cheese
- 1/2 cup of whole milk
- A pinch of ground cinnamon
- Whipped cream, to top

Instructions:

1. Prepare 2 shots of espresso.
2. Heat a small saucepan over low heat and add the cream cheese and milk. Heat until the cream cheese is melted.
3. Remove from heat and stir in the cinnamon and strawberry syrup.
4. Pour espresso into a cup and top with the cream cheese-strawberry mixture.
5. Garnish with whipped cream and a few slices of fresh strawberry, if desired.

Nutrition information: Each cup of Strawberry Cheesecake Latte contains 158 calories, 8.7g fat, 13.3g sugar, and 4.9g protein.

76. Brown Sugar Caramel Latte

A sweet and creamy brown sugar caramel latte, this indulgent beverage will make you want for more! With a simple yet heavenly combination of creamy milk, aromatic espresso and brown sugar caramel, this latte will tantalize your taste buds and will sure be a crowd pleaser.
Serving: 4
Preparation time: 10 minutes
Ready time: 10 minutes

Ingredients:
- 2 cups of milk, preferably whole
- 2-3 tablespoons of brown sugar caramel
- 1-2 shots of espresso
- Ice, as needed
- Optional: whipped cream and cinnamon to top

Instructions:
1. Heat milk in a saucepan over low-medium heat.
2. Put brown sugar caramel into the saucepan and stir to combine.
3. Once the milk is hot, pour it into a blender and mix for a few seconds.
4. Put the espresso shots into the milk mixture and blend again for another few seconds.
5. Pour the mixture into four mugs and add ice.
6. Optionally top with whipped cream and cinnamon.

Nutrition information: per serving (1 cup): 140 calories; 10g fat; 6g carbohydrates; 4g protein.

77. Cookies and Cream Latte

This delicious Cookies and Cream Latte is made with a generous blend of dark chocolate syrup, espresso, and foamed milk and finished with an Oreo cookie. A decadent treat that is sure to leave you with a smile!
Serving: 1
Preparation Time: 5 minutes
Ready Time: 5 minutes

Ingredients:
- 1/4 cup dark chocolate syrup
- 1 cup espresso
- 1 cup foamed milk
- 1 Oreo cookie

Instructions:
1. In a mug, whisk together the dark chocolate syrup and espresso until combined.
2. Heat the foamed milk and pour it into the mug. Mix until combined.
3. Top with an Oreo cookie.
4. Enjoy!

Nutrition information:
Calories: 165 kcal, Carbohydrates: 28 g, Protein: 3 g, Fat: 4 g, Saturated Fat: 2 g, Cholesterol: 6 mg, Sodium: 110 mg, Potassium: 47 mg, Fiber: 1 g, Sugar: 20 g, Vitamin A: 72 IU, Vitamin C: 0 mg, Calcium: 67 mg, Iron: 1 mg

78. Mocha Cookie Crumble

Indulge in the rich and decadent flavors of our Mocha Cookie Crumble. This delightful treat combines the irresistible combination of chocolate, coffee, and crunchy cookies. Perfect for any occasion, this dessert is sure to satisfy your sweet tooth and leave you craving for more.

Serving: 12 cookies
Preparation time: 15 minutes
Ready time: 1 hour

Ingredients:
- 1 cup all-purpose flour
- 1/4 cup unsweetened cocoa powder
- 1/2 teaspoon baking soda
- 1/4 teaspoon salt
- 1/2 cup unsalted butter, softened
- 1/2 cup granulated sugar
- 1/2 cup brown sugar
- 1 large egg
- 1 teaspoon vanilla extract
- 1 tablespoon instant coffee granules
- 1 cup semisweet chocolate chips
- 1/2 cup crushed chocolate cookies

Instructions:
1. Preheat your oven to 350°F (175°C) and line a baking sheet with parchment paper.
2. In a medium-sized bowl, whisk together the flour, cocoa powder, baking soda, and salt. Set aside.
3. In a separate large bowl, cream together the softened butter, granulated sugar, and brown sugar until light and fluffy.
4. Add the egg and vanilla extract to the butter mixture and mix until well combined.
5. Dissolve the instant coffee granules in 1 tablespoon of hot water, then add it to the butter mixture and mix well.
6. Gradually add the dry Ingredients to the wet Ingredients, mixing until just combined.
7. Fold in the chocolate chips and crushed chocolate cookies, ensuring they are evenly distributed throughout the dough.
8. Using a cookie scoop or tablespoon, drop rounded portions of dough onto the prepared baking sheet, spacing them about 2 inches apart.
9. Bake for 10-12 minutes, or until the edges are set and the centers are slightly soft.
10. Allow the cookies to cool on the baking sheet for 5 minutes, then transfer them to a wire rack to cool completely.

Nutrition information per Serving: - Calories: 220
- Total Fat: 11g
- Saturated Fat: 7g
- Cholesterol: 30mg
- Sodium: 110mg
- Total Carbohydrate: 30g
- Dietary Fiber: 2g
- Sugars: 19g
- Protein: 3g

Note: Nutrition information may vary depending on the specific Ingredients and brands used.

79. Chocolate Coconut Latte

Chocolate Coconut Latte is a deliciously decadent drink that is the perfect way to sip your way into the weekend. Combining creamy coconut milk, dark chocolate, and espresso, this latte is sure to be a hit with coffee lovers of all ages.

Serving: 1
Preparation time: 5 minutes
Ready time: 5 minutes

Ingredients:
-1/2 cup brewed espresso
-1/3 cup coconut milk
-1/2 teaspoon cocoa powder
-1 tablespoon dark chocolate chips
-1 teaspoon honey (optional)

Instructions:
1. In a saucepan, heat the coconut milk over medium heat until it is steaming.
2. Add the espresso, cocoa powder, dark chocolate chips, and honey (if desired) and stir until all Ingredients are well combined.
3. Pour into a cup and enjoy.

Nutrition information: calories", 180; fat, 9.5g; saturated fat, 8.3g; carbohydrates, 15.1g; protein, 1.9g; cholesterol, 0mg; sodium, 65mg; sugars, 10.6g.

80. Cherry Almond Latte

Cherry Almond Latte is a delightful and refreshing beverage that combines the flavors of sweet cherries and nutty almonds with the richness of a latte. This drink is perfect for those who enjoy a hint of fruitiness in their coffee. Whether you're looking for a morning pick-me-up or a cozy evening treat, this Cherry Almond Latte is sure to satisfy your cravings.
Serving: 1 Serving: Preparation time: 5 minutes
Ready time: 10 minutes

Ingredients:
- 1 cup of strong brewed coffee
- 1/2 cup of almond milk
- 1 tablespoon of cherry syrup
- 1/4 teaspoon of almond extract
- Whipped cream (optional)
- Sliced almonds (for garnish)

Instructions:
1. Brew a cup of strong coffee using your preferred method. Set it aside.
2. In a small saucepan, heat the almond milk over medium heat until it starts to steam. Do not let it boil.
3. Once the almond milk is steaming, remove it from the heat and whisk in the cherry syrup and almond extract until well combined.
4. Pour the cherry almond mixture into a blender and blend on high speed for about 30 seconds until frothy.
5. Pour the frothy mixture into a large mug or latte glass.
6. Slowly pour the brewed coffee into the mug, allowing it to mix with the cherry almond mixture.
7. If desired, top the latte with a dollop of whipped cream and sprinkle with sliced almonds for an extra touch of indulgence.
8. Serve the Cherry Almond Latte hot and enjoy!

Nutrition information:
- Calories: 120
- Fat: 4g
- Carbohydrates: 18g
- Protein: 2g
- Sugar: 12g
- Fiber: 1g

Note: Nutrition information may vary depending on the specific brands and quantities of Ingredients used.

81. Mint Chocolate Latte

Indulge in the refreshing combination of mint and chocolate with this delightful Mint Chocolate Latte recipe. This creamy and aromatic beverage is perfect for those cozy evenings or as a special treat to start your day. With just a few simple Ingredients, you can create a delicious minty twist on your regular latte.

Serving: 1 Serving: Preparation time: 5 minutes
Ready time: 10 minutes

Ingredients:
- 1 cup of milk
- 1 tablespoon of cocoa powder
- 1 tablespoon of sugar
- 1/4 teaspoon of peppermint extract
- 1 shot of espresso or 1/2 cup of strong brewed coffee
- Whipped cream (optional)
- Chocolate shavings (optional)

Instructions:
1. In a small saucepan, heat the milk over medium heat until it starts to steam. Do not let it boil.
2. In a separate bowl, whisk together the cocoa powder and sugar until well combined.
3. Slowly add the cocoa powder mixture to the steaming milk, whisking constantly to prevent any lumps from forming.
4. Stir in the peppermint extract and continue to heat the mixture until it reaches your desired temperature.

5. Meanwhile, prepare your espresso or strong brewed coffee.
6. Pour the espresso or coffee into a mug and slowly pour the mint chocolate milk over it, stirring gently to combine.
7. If desired, top with whipped cream and sprinkle with chocolate shavings for an extra touch of indulgence.
8. Serve hot and enjoy!

Nutrition information:
- Calories: 150
- Fat: 5g
- Carbohydrates: 20g
- Protein: 8g
- Fiber: 2g
- Sugar: 16g
- Sodium: 100mg

Note: Nutrition information may vary depending on the specific brands and quantities of Ingredients used.

82. Caramel Apple Latte

Indulge in the cozy flavors of fall with our delicious Caramel Apple Latte. This warm and comforting beverage combines the sweetness of caramel and the tartness of apples, creating a delightful treat that will satisfy your cravings. Whether you enjoy it as a morning pick-me-up or a soothing evening drink, this latte is sure to become your new favorite fall beverage.

Serving: 1 Serving: Preparation time: 5 minutes
Ready time: 10 minutes

Ingredients:
- 1 cup of milk
- 1/4 cup of strong brewed coffee or espresso
- 2 tablespoons of caramel sauce
- 1 tablespoon of apple syrup
- Whipped cream (optional)
- Cinnamon powder (optional)

Instructions:

1. In a small saucepan, heat the milk over medium heat until hot but not boiling.
2. In a mug, combine the brewed coffee or espresso, caramel sauce, and apple syrup. Stir well to combine.
3. Pour the hot milk into the mug, stirring gently to mix all the Ingredients together.
4. If desired, top with whipped cream and a sprinkle of cinnamon powder for extra flavor and presentation.
5. Serve immediately and enjoy the warm and comforting flavors of the Caramel Apple Latte.

Nutrition information:
- Calories: 180
- Fat: 6g
- Carbohydrates: 26g
- Protein: 8g
- Sugar: 20g
- Fiber: 0g
- Sodium: 120mg

Note: Nutrition information may vary depending on the specific brands and quantities of Ingredients used.

83. Blueberry Muffin Latte

Indulge in the delightful combination of a classic blueberry muffin and a creamy latte with our Blueberry Muffin Latte recipe. This comforting beverage is the perfect way to start your day or enjoy as a mid-afternoon treat. With the sweet and tangy flavors of blueberries and the rich creaminess of a latte, this drink is sure to satisfy your cravings.
Serving: 1 Serving: Preparation time: 5 minutes
Ready time: 10 minutes

Ingredients:
- 1 cup milk
- 1/4 cup fresh or frozen blueberries
- 1 tablespoon sugar
- 1/2 teaspoon vanilla extract
- 1/4 teaspoon ground cinnamon

- 1/4 cup brewed espresso or strong coffee
- Whipped cream (optional)
- Fresh blueberries for garnish (optional)

Instructions:
1. In a small saucepan, heat the milk over medium heat until hot but not boiling. Stir occasionally to prevent scorching.
2. In a blender, combine the blueberries, sugar, vanilla extract, and ground cinnamon. Blend until smooth.
3. Pour the blueberry mixture into the saucepan with the hot milk. Whisk well to combine.
4. Add the brewed espresso or strong coffee to the saucepan and whisk again until everything is well mixed.
5. Continue heating the mixture over medium heat until it reaches your desired temperature. Be careful not to let it boil.
6. Once heated, remove the saucepan from the heat and pour the Blueberry Muffin Latte into a mug.
7. If desired, top with whipped cream and garnish with fresh blueberries.
8. Serve immediately and enjoy!

Nutrition information:
- Calories: 180
- Fat: 4g
- Carbohydrates: 28g
- Protein: 8g
- Fiber: 2g
- Sugar: 24g
- Sodium: 100mg

Note: Nutrition information may vary depending on the specific brands and quantities of Ingredients used.

84. Gingerbread White Mocha

Gingerbread White Mocha is a delightful and cozy beverage that combines the flavors of gingerbread and creamy white chocolate. This festive drink is perfect for the holiday season or any time you want to indulge in a warm and comforting treat. With a hint of spice and a touch of sweetness, this gingerbread white mocha is sure to become a favorite.

Serving: 1
Preparation time: 5 minutes
Ready time: 10 minutes

Ingredients:
- 1 cup of milk
- 2 tablespoons of white chocolate chips
- 1 shot of espresso or 1/2 cup of strong brewed coffee
- 1 tablespoon of gingerbread syrup
- Whipped cream, for topping
- Ground cinnamon or nutmeg, for garnish (optional)

Instructions:
1. In a small saucepan, heat the milk over medium heat until hot but not boiling. Stir occasionally to prevent scorching.
2. Once the milk is hot, add the white chocolate chips and stir until melted and well combined.
3. In a separate mug, prepare the espresso or strong brewed coffee.
4. Pour the gingerbread syrup into the mug with the coffee and stir to combine.
5. Slowly pour the hot milk and white chocolate mixture into the mug with the coffee and syrup. Stir gently to combine all the flavors.
6. Top with whipped cream and sprinkle with ground cinnamon or nutmeg, if desired.
7. Serve immediately and enjoy the warm and comforting flavors of gingerbread white mocha.

Nutrition information:
- Calories: 250
- Fat: 10g
- Carbohydrates: 30g
- Protein: 8g
- Sugar: 25g
- Fiber: 1g
- Sodium: 100mg

Note: Nutrition information may vary depending on the specific brands and quantities of Ingredients used.

85. Maple Bacon Latte

Indulge in the perfect blend of sweet and savory with our Maple Bacon Latte. This unique beverage combines the rich flavors of maple syrup and crispy bacon with a smooth and creamy latte base. It's the ultimate treat for bacon lovers and coffee enthusiasts alike. Get ready to savor every sip of this deliciously comforting drink!
Serving: 1 Serving: Preparation time: 5 minutes
Ready time: 10 minutes

Ingredients:
- 1 cup of strong brewed coffee
- 1 cup of milk
- 2 tablespoons of maple syrup
- 2 strips of bacon, cooked and crumbled
- Whipped cream (optional, for garnish)
- Maple syrup (optional, for drizzling)

Instructions:
1. Brew a cup of strong coffee using your preferred method. Set aside.
2. In a small saucepan, heat the milk over medium heat until hot but not boiling. Remove from heat.
3. In a separate pan, cook the bacon until crispy. Once cooked, transfer to a paper towel-lined plate to drain excess grease. Crumble the bacon into small pieces and set aside.
4. In a microwave-safe bowl, warm the maple syrup for about 20 seconds until it becomes slightly runny.
5. In a large mug, combine the brewed coffee, hot milk, and warmed maple syrup. Stir well to combine.
6. Top the latte with whipped cream, if desired, and sprinkle the crumbled bacon on top.
7. For an extra touch of sweetness, drizzle some additional maple syrup over the whipped cream.
8. Serve the Maple Bacon Latte hot and enjoy!

Nutrition information:
- Calories: 200
- Fat: 8g
- Carbohydrates: 25g
- Protein: 8g

- Sugar: 18g
- Fiber: 0g
- Sodium: 200mg

Note: Nutrition information may vary depending on the specific brands and quantities of Ingredients used.

86. Chocolate Peanut Butter Latte

Satisfy your sweet tooth with this creamy and chocolaty Chocolate Peanut Butter Latte. A flavor combination never tasted so good!
Serving: 1
Preparation time: 5 minutes
Ready time: 5 minutes

Ingredients:
- 2 cups of brewed coffee
- 2 tablespoons creamy peanut butter
- 2 tablespoons cocoa powder
- 4 tablespoons of warm milk
- 2 tablespoons of sugar

Instructions:
1. In a blender, combine the brewed coffee, peanut butter, cocoa powder and warm milk.
2. Blend until the mixture is smooth and creamy.
3. Add the sugar and blend until combined.
4. Pour the latte into a mug and enjoy.

Nutrition information: Calories - 470, Fat - 16g, Carbohydrates - 66g, Protein - 14g

87. Spiced Pumpkin Chai Latte

Spiced pumpkin chai latte is a delicious twist on the classic chai drink. This creamy, frothy latte is perfect for a cozy, autumn day.
Serving: 1
Preparation time: 5 minutes

Ready time: 5 minutes

Ingredients:
- 1/2 cup strong brewed chai tea
- 1/2 teaspoon pumpkin pie spice
- 2 teaspoons pure pumpkin puree (or to taste)
- 2 tablespoons of sugar (or other sweetener)
- 1/2 cup milk of your choice

Instructions:
1. In a small pot, bring the chai tea to simmer over medium heat;
2. Add the pumpkin pie spice and pumpkin puree, stirring until the mixture is combined and just beginning to boil;
3. Reduce the heat to low and whisk in the sugar and the milk. Stir until combined and warmed through;
4. Pour the mixture into a mug and top with foam or whipped cream for extra decadence.

Nutrition information:
- Calories: 110
- Total Fat: 4 g
- Sodium: 37 mg
- Total Carbohydrates: 16 g
- Sugars: 15 g
- Protein: 4 g

88. Eggnog Latte

Eggnog Latte is a delightful and creamy beverage that combines the rich flavors of eggnog with the boldness of espresso. This festive drink is perfect for the holiday season or any time you want to indulge in a cozy and comforting treat. With just a few simple Ingredients, you can whip up this delicious Eggnog Latte in no time.
Serving: 1 Serving: Preparation time: 5 minutes
Ready time: 10 minutes

Ingredients:
- 1 cup of strong brewed coffee or 2 shots of espresso

- 1 cup of eggnog
- 1/4 cup of milk
- 1 tablespoon of sugar
- 1/2 teaspoon of vanilla extract
- A pinch of ground nutmeg (for garnish)

Instructions:
1. In a small saucepan, heat the eggnog and milk over medium heat until hot but not boiling. Stir occasionally to prevent scorching.
2. Meanwhile, brew a cup of strong coffee or prepare 2 shots of espresso using your preferred method.
3. In a large mug, combine the hot coffee or espresso with the sugar and vanilla extract. Stir until the sugar is dissolved.
4. Slowly pour the hot eggnog and milk mixture into the mug, stirring gently to combine.
5. Sprinkle a pinch of ground nutmeg on top for garnish.
6. Serve the Eggnog Latte hot and enjoy!

Nutrition information:
- Calories: 250
- Fat: 10g
- Carbohydrates: 30g
- Protein: 8g
- Sugar: 25g
- Sodium: 100mg

Note: Nutrition information may vary depending on the brand of eggnog and milk used.

89. Cinnamon Hot Chocolate

Cinnamon Hot Chocolate is a delightful and comforting beverage that combines the rich flavors of chocolate with a hint of warm cinnamon. This indulgent drink is perfect for cozy evenings or as a special treat during the holiday season. With just a few simple Ingredients, you can whip up a delicious mug of Cinnamon Hot Chocolate in no time.
Serving: 2 servings
Preparation time: 5 minutes
Ready time: 10 minutes

Ingredients:
- 2 cups of milk
- 2 tablespoons of unsweetened cocoa powder
- 2 tablespoons of granulated sugar
- 1/2 teaspoon of ground cinnamon
- 1/4 teaspoon of vanilla extract
- Whipped cream (optional, for garnish)
- Ground cinnamon (optional, for garnish)

Instructions:
1. In a small saucepan, heat the milk over medium heat until it starts to steam. Do not let it boil.
2. In a separate bowl, whisk together the cocoa powder, sugar, and ground cinnamon until well combined.
3. Slowly add the cocoa mixture to the steaming milk, whisking constantly to prevent any lumps from forming.
4. Continue to heat the mixture, stirring occasionally, until it reaches your desired temperature.
5. Remove the saucepan from the heat and stir in the vanilla extract.
6. Pour the Cinnamon Hot Chocolate into mugs and garnish with whipped cream and a sprinkle of ground cinnamon, if desired.
7. Serve immediately and enjoy!

Nutrition information per Serving: - Calories: 150
- Fat: 4g
- Saturated Fat: 2.5g
- Cholesterol: 15mg
- Sodium: 80mg
- Carbohydrates: 25g
- Fiber: 2g
- Sugar: 20g
- Protein: 8g

Note: Nutrition information may vary depending on the specific Ingredients and brands used.

90. White Hot Chocolate

White hot chocolate is a delicious and creamy twist on the classic hot chocolate. Made with white chocolate and warm milk, this indulgent beverage is perfect for cozy winter nights or as a special treat any time of the year. With just a few simple Ingredients and easy steps, you can whip up a comforting cup of white hot chocolate in no time.
Serving: 2 servings
Preparation time: 5 minutes
Ready time: 10 minutes

Ingredients:
- 2 cups whole milk
- 1 cup white chocolate chips
- 1/2 teaspoon vanilla extract
- Whipped cream, for topping (optional)
- Sprinkles or grated white chocolate, for garnish (optional)

Instructions:
1. In a small saucepan, heat the milk over medium heat until it starts to steam. Do not let it boil.
2. Add the white chocolate chips to the saucepan and stir continuously until they are completely melted and the mixture is smooth.
3. Remove the saucepan from heat and stir in the vanilla extract.
4. Pour the white hot chocolate into mugs and top with whipped cream, if desired.
5. Garnish with sprinkles or grated white chocolate, if desired.
6. Serve immediately and enjoy!

Nutrition information per Serving: - Calories: 350
- Fat: 20g
- Saturated Fat: 12g
- Cholesterol: 30mg
- Sodium: 100mg
- Carbohydrates: 35g
- Fiber: 0g
- Sugar: 34g
- Protein: 8g

Note: Nutrition information may vary depending on the brands of Ingredients used.

91. Raspberry Hot Chocolate

Indulge in the rich and comforting flavors of Raspberry Hot Chocolate. This delightful beverage combines the sweetness of raspberries with the smoothness of hot chocolate, creating a perfect treat for those chilly winter evenings. Whether you're snuggled up by the fireplace or hosting a cozy gathering, this recipe is sure to warm your heart and satisfy your sweet tooth.

Serving: 2 servings
Preparation time: 5 minutes
Ready time: 10 minutes

Ingredients:
- 2 cups milk
- 1/2 cup fresh or frozen raspberries
- 2 tablespoons unsweetened cocoa powder
- 2 tablespoons sugar (adjust to taste)
- 1/4 teaspoon vanilla extract
- Whipped cream, for garnish (optional)
- Fresh raspberries, for garnish (optional)

Instructions:
1. In a small saucepan, heat the milk over medium heat until it starts to steam. Do not let it boil.
2. Add the raspberries to the saucepan and stir gently. Let the mixture simmer for about 5 minutes, allowing the raspberries to soften and release their flavors.
3. Using a fine-mesh strainer or cheesecloth, strain the raspberry mixture into a clean saucepan, discarding the solids.
4. Place the saucepan with the strained raspberry milk back on the stove over low heat.
5. Whisk in the cocoa powder, sugar, and vanilla extract until well combined and the mixture is smooth.
6. Continue to heat the hot chocolate, stirring occasionally, until it reaches your desired temperature.
7. Once heated, remove the hot chocolate from the heat and pour it into mugs.
8. If desired, top each mug with a dollop of whipped cream and a few fresh raspberries for garnish.

9. Serve immediately and enjoy the comforting flavors of Raspberry Hot Chocolate.

Nutrition information (per serving):
- Calories: 180
- Fat: 5g
- Carbohydrates: 28g
- Protein: 8g
- Fiber: 4g
- Sugar: 22g
- Sodium: 100mg

92. Peppermint Hot Chocolate

Rich and creamy peppermint hot chocolate is the perfect winter cozy drink! Enjoy the creamy hot chocolate with a hint of minty peppermint and warm up on a cold day. Serving: 4 Preparation Time: 5 minutes Ready Time: 10 minutes

Ingredients:
- 2 cups of whole milk
- 2 tablespoons of cocoa powder
- 2 tablespoons of granulated sugar
- ¼ teaspoon of salt
- ½ teaspoon of pure vanilla extract
- ½ teaspoon of peppermint extract
- Whipped cream and peppermint candy pieces for topping (optional)

Instructions:
1. In a small saucepan, whisk together milk, cocoa powder, sugar, and salt until combined.
2. Heat the mixture over medium heat for a few minutes, whisking often.
3. When the mixture starts to steam and bubble slightly, remove from heat and whisk in the vanilla and peppermint extracts until combined.
4. Pour the hot chocolate into mugs and top with whipped cream and peppermint candy pieces if desired.

Nutrition information: Calories: 200kcal, Carbohydrates: 26g, Protein: 5g, Fat: 9g, Saturated Fat: 5g, Cholesterol: 25mg, Sodium: 140mg, Potassium: 230mg, Fiber: 1g, Sugar: 21g, Vitamin A: 310IU, Calcium: 140mg, Iron: 0.8mg.

93. Nutella Hot Chocolate

Indulge in the ultimate comfort drink with this delicious Nutella Hot Chocolate recipe. Made with the creamy goodness of Nutella and rich chocolate, this warm beverage is perfect for cozy evenings or as a sweet treat during the colder months. With just a few simple Ingredients and easy steps, you can whip up this delightful drink in no time.
Serving: 2 servings
Preparation time: 5 minutes
Ready time: 10 minutes

Ingredients:
- 2 cups of milk
- 4 tablespoons of Nutella
- 2 tablespoons of unsweetened cocoa powder
- 2 tablespoons of sugar (adjust to taste)
- 1/2 teaspoon of vanilla extract
- Whipped cream (optional, for topping)
- Chocolate shavings (optional, for garnish)

Instructions:
1. In a small saucepan, heat the milk over medium heat until it starts to steam. Do not let it boil.
2. Add the Nutella, cocoa powder, sugar, and vanilla extract to the saucepan. Whisk continuously until the Nutella has melted and all the Ingredients are well combined.
3. Continue to heat the mixture, whisking occasionally, until it reaches your desired temperature.
4. Once heated, remove the saucepan from the heat and pour the Nutella hot chocolate into mugs.
5. If desired, top each mug with a dollop of whipped cream and sprinkle with chocolate shavings.
6. Serve immediately and enjoy!

Nutrition information per Serving: - Calories: 250
- Fat: 10g
- Saturated Fat: 6g
- Cholesterol: 20mg
- Sodium: 100mg
- Carbohydrates: 35g
- Fiber: 2g
- Sugar: 30g
- Protein: 8g

Note: Nutrition information may vary depending on the specific brands and quantities of Ingredients used.

94. Salted Caramel Hot Chocolate

Indulge in the rich and comforting flavors of Salted Caramel Hot Chocolate. This delightful beverage combines the sweetness of caramel with a hint of salt, creating a perfect balance of flavors. Whether you're looking for a cozy treat on a chilly day or a special drink to enjoy with friends and family, this recipe is sure to satisfy your cravings.

Serving: 2 servings
Preparation time: 5 minutes
Ready time: 10 minutes

Ingredients:
- 2 cups milk
- 2 tablespoons unsweetened cocoa powder
- 2 tablespoons granulated sugar
- 1/4 teaspoon salt
- 1/4 cup caramel sauce
- Whipped cream, for topping
- Sea salt, for garnish

Instructions:
1. In a small saucepan, heat the milk over medium heat until hot but not boiling. Stir occasionally to prevent scorching.
2. In a separate bowl, whisk together the cocoa powder, sugar, and salt until well combined.

3. Slowly add the cocoa mixture to the hot milk, whisking constantly to ensure it dissolves completely.
4. Continue to heat the mixture, stirring occasionally, until it reaches a gentle simmer.
5. Remove the saucepan from the heat and stir in the caramel sauce until fully incorporated.
6. Pour the hot chocolate into mugs and top with whipped cream.
7. Sprinkle a pinch of sea salt over the whipped cream for an extra touch of flavor.
8. Serve immediately and enjoy!

Nutrition information:
- Calories: 250
- Fat: 8g
- Carbohydrates: 40g
- Protein: 8g
- Fiber: 2g
- Sugar: 32g
- Sodium: 350mg

Note: Nutrition information may vary depending on the specific Ingredients and brands used.

95. Caramel Apple Hot Chocolate

Caramel Apple Hot Chocolate is a delightful and comforting beverage that combines the flavors of caramel, apple, and rich hot chocolate. This indulgent treat is perfect for chilly evenings or as a special treat during the holiday season. The combination of sweet caramel, tart apple, and creamy hot chocolate creates a delicious and warming drink that will surely satisfy your sweet tooth.
Serving: 2 servings
Preparation time: 5 minutes
Ready time: 10 minutes

Ingredients:
- 2 cups of milk
- 2 tablespoons of cocoa powder
- 2 tablespoons of caramel sauce

- 1/4 cup of chopped apple
- Whipped cream, for topping
- Caramel drizzle, for garnish (optional)

Instructions:
1. In a small saucepan, heat the milk over medium heat until it starts to steam. Do not let it boil.
2. In a separate bowl, whisk together the cocoa powder and caramel sauce until well combined.
3. Slowly pour the cocoa powder mixture into the saucepan with the steaming milk, whisking constantly to prevent any lumps from forming.
4. Continue to heat the mixture, stirring occasionally, until it is hot and well blended.
5. Add the chopped apple to the hot chocolate and let it simmer for an additional 2-3 minutes, allowing the flavors to meld together.
6. Remove the hot chocolate from the heat and pour it into mugs.
7. Top each mug with a dollop of whipped cream and drizzle with caramel sauce for an extra touch of sweetness.
8. Serve the Caramel Apple Hot Chocolate immediately and enjoy!

Nutrition information per Serving: - Calories: 220
- Fat: 8g
- Carbohydrates: 32g
- Protein: 8g
- Fiber: 3g
- Sugar: 24g
- Sodium: 120mg

Note: Nutrition information may vary depending on the specific brands and quantities of Ingredients used.

96. Mocha Hot Chocolate

Rich and creamy, this heavenly Mocha Hot Chocolate is the perfect drink for the winter season! Serve with your favorite toppings for an extra special treat.
Serving: 4
Preparation time: 10 minutes
Ready time: 10 minutes

Ingredients:
- 3 tablespoons of unsweetened cocoa powder
- 2 tablespoons of sugar
- 2 teaspoons of instant coffee
- 3 cups of milk
- 2 tablespoons of semi-sweet chocolate chips
- Whipped cream, marshmallows (optional for serving)

Instructions:
1. In a medium-sized saucepan, whisk together cocoa powder, sugar, and instant coffee.
2. Gradually pour in the milk while whisking the mixture until everything is well combined.
3. Heat the mixture over medium-high heat, stirring constantly until it is combined and hot.
4. Remove the pot from the heat and stir in the chocolate chips until they are melted and the mixture is smooth.
5. Divide the hot chocolate among four mugs and top with whipped cream and marshmallows, if desired.

Nutrition information: per serving (without optional toppings):
Calories: 156 kcal
Carbohydrates: 22 g
Protein: 8 g
Fat: 4 g

97. Pumpkin Spice Hot Chocolate

Pumpkin Spice Hot Chocolate is the perfect cozy drink for chilly autumn evenings. This delightful blend of rich chocolate and warm pumpkin spice will surely satisfy your sweet tooth and warm you up from the inside out. Whether you're enjoying it by the fireplace or as a treat after a long day, this indulgent beverage is sure to become a fall favorite.
Serving: 2 servings
Preparation time: 5 minutes
Ready time: 10 minutes

Ingredients:
- 2 cups milk
- 1/4 cup pumpkin puree
- 2 tablespoons unsweetened cocoa powder
- 2 tablespoons granulated sugar
- 1/2 teaspoon pumpkin pie spice
- 1/4 teaspoon vanilla extract
- Whipped cream, for topping (optional)
- Cinnamon, for garnish (optional)

Instructions:
1. In a small saucepan, heat the milk over medium heat until hot but not boiling. Stir occasionally to prevent scorching.
2. In a separate bowl, whisk together the pumpkin puree, cocoa powder, sugar, pumpkin pie spice, and vanilla extract until well combined.
3. Slowly pour the pumpkin mixture into the hot milk, whisking constantly to ensure it is fully incorporated.
4. Continue to heat the mixture over medium heat, stirring occasionally, until it reaches your desired temperature.
5. Once heated, remove the saucepan from the heat and pour the hot chocolate into mugs.
6. If desired, top each mug with a dollop of whipped cream and sprinkle with a pinch of cinnamon for added flavor and presentation.
7. Serve immediately and enjoy!

Nutrition information:
- Calories: 180
- Fat: 4g
- Carbohydrates: 30g
- Protein: 8g
- Fiber: 4g
- Sugar: 24g
- Sodium: 100mg

Note: Nutrition information may vary depending on the specific Ingredients and brands used.

98. Spiced Chai Hot Chocolate

Spiced Chai Hot Chocolate is a delightful blend of traditional Indian spices and rich chocolate, creating a warm and comforting beverage perfect for chilly days. This fusion of flavors will surely satisfy your cravings for both chai tea and hot chocolate.

Serving: 2 servings
Preparation time: 5 minutes
Ready time: 10 minutes

Ingredients:
- 2 cups milk
- 2 chai tea bags
- 2 tablespoons unsweetened cocoa powder
- 2 tablespoons granulated sugar
- 1/2 teaspoon ground cinnamon
- 1/4 teaspoon ground cardamom
- 1/4 teaspoon ground ginger
- 1/8 teaspoon ground cloves
- Whipped cream (optional, for garnish)
- Ground cinnamon (optional, for garnish)

Instructions:
1. In a small saucepan, heat the milk over medium heat until it starts to steam. Do not let it boil.
2. Add the chai tea bags to the milk and let them steep for 5 minutes.
3. Remove the tea bags and discard them.
4. In a separate bowl, whisk together the cocoa powder, sugar, cinnamon, cardamom, ginger, and cloves.
5. Slowly add the cocoa mixture to the milk, whisking constantly to ensure it is well combined.
6. Continue to heat the mixture over medium heat, stirring occasionally, until it is hot and well blended.
7. Remove from heat and pour the spiced chai hot chocolate into mugs.
8. If desired, top each mug with a dollop of whipped cream and a sprinkle of ground cinnamon.
9. Serve immediately and enjoy!

Nutrition information (per serving):
- Calories: 150
- Fat: 5g
- Saturated Fat: 3g

- Cholesterol: 15mg
- Sodium: 80mg
- Carbohydrates: 22g
- Fiber: 2g
- Sugar: 17g
- Protein: 7g
- Vitamin D: 2mcg
- Calcium: 250mg
- Iron: 1mg

99. Almond Joy Hot Chocolate

Almond Joy Hot Chocolate is a creamy, indulgent winter warmer that is sure to bring joy to all warm chocolate lovers.
Serving: 2
Preparation time: 3 minutes
Ready time: 7 minutes

Ingredients:
- 2 cups of milk
- ½ tbsp of cocoa powder
- 2 tsp of almond extract
- 2 tsp of turbinado sugar
- 2 tsp of Toasted Coconut
- ¼ tsp of Sea Salt

Instructions:
1. Heat the milk in a saucepan over low heat until small bubbles start to form at the side.
2. Pull off the heat and stir in the cocoa powder, almond extract, sugar, toasted coconut, and salt.
3. Place the pan back on the heat over medium heat and whisk until the hot chocolate is smooth and creamy with no lumps.
4. Once hot chocolate has reached desired temperature, pour into two mugs and serve immediately with desired toppings.

Nutrition information
- Calories: 140

- Fat: 7g
- Carbs: 15g
- Protein: 5g

100. Cookies and Cream Hot Chocolate

Try out this delicious winter warmer – Cookies and Cream Hot Chocolate. This heavenly combination of cookies, cream and blended hot chocolate will be a hit with everyone!
Serving: Serves 4
Preparation time: 5 minutes
Ready time: 10 minutes

Ingredients:
- 2 cups of semi-skimmed milk
- 2 tablespoons of sugar
- 2 teaspoons of vanilla extract
- 2 tablespoons of cocoa powder
- 2 tablespoons of cream biscuits, crumbled
- 4 tablespoons of whipped cream

Instructions:
1. Place the milk in a small saucepan over a low heat.
2. Once warm, add the sugar, cream biscuits, cocoa powder and vanilla extract.
3. Whisk constantly.
4. Once the mixture has heated through and is beginning to bubble, turn off the heat.
5. Divide the mixture between four mugs and add the whipped cream.
6. Serve.

Nutrition information: Per serving, Calories: 103, Carbohydrates: 15g, Protein: 3g, Fat: 4.5g, Sodium: 68mg

101. S'mores Hot Chocolate

S'mores Hot Chocolate is a delightful and indulgent treat that combines the classic flavors of s'mores with a rich and creamy hot chocolate. This comforting beverage is perfect for cozy nights by the fire or as a special treat during the holiday season. With just a few simple Ingredients, you can whip up this delicious drink in no time.

Serving: 2 servings
Preparation time: 5 minutes
Ready time: 10 minutes

Ingredients:
- 2 cups milk
- 2 tablespoons cocoa powder
- 2 tablespoons granulated sugar
- 1/4 cup chocolate chips
- 1/4 cup mini marshmallows
- 2 graham crackers, crushed
- Whipped cream, for topping (optional)

Instructions:
1. In a small saucepan, heat the milk over medium heat until hot but not boiling.
2. In a separate bowl, whisk together the cocoa powder and sugar until well combined.
3. Gradually add the cocoa mixture to the hot milk, whisking constantly until smooth and well blended.
4. Stir in the chocolate chips until melted and fully incorporated into the hot chocolate.
5. Remove the saucepan from heat and pour the hot chocolate into two mugs.
6. Top each mug with mini marshmallows and sprinkle with crushed graham crackers.
7. If desired, add a dollop of whipped cream on top.
8. Serve immediately and enjoy!

Nutrition information:
- Calories: 250
- Fat: 10g
- Carbohydrates: 35g
- Protein: 8g
- Fiber: 3g

- Sugar: 25g
- Sodium: 100mg

Note: Nutrition information may vary depending on the brands of Ingredients used.

CONCLUSION

Cooking can be fun and rewarding. Whether you're a seasoned barista or just starting out, Barista's Coffee Creations: 101 Recipes and Expert Tips is the perfect book to get you on your way. With simple steps and detailed instructions, it'll have you creating gourmet coffee beverages in no time.

Not only do the recipes provide a great base, but the expert tips help to take your drinks to the next level. From grinding your own beans to specialized milk frothing techniques, this cookbook has you covered. You'll even find ideas for flavored syrups and toppings to make your drinks extra special.

Whether you're looking to whip up a perfect cup of espresso for yourself or make delicious coffee deserts for your friends and family, Barista's Coffee Creations: 101 Recipes and Expert Tips has you covered. With high-quality recipes and essential insider tips, this book will have you serving up your own gourmet creations in no time. Plus, with such a wide variety of recipes, this cookbook can provide tasty inspiration for years to come.

This cookbook is a great resource to get the barista in you up and running in no time. Whether you're a professional or an amateur barista, you'll find something for everyone in this book. From detailed recipes to expert tips, this cookbook celebrates the art of coffee making—and all the creativity that comes with it. So, grab yourself a copy of Barista's Coffee Creations: 101 Recipes and Expert Tips and get started. You won't regret it.

In conclusion, Barista's Coffee Creations: 101 Recipes and Expert Tips is sure to bring out your inner barista. Whether you're a professional or an amateur, you'll find something for everyone in this cookbook. With its high-quality recipes and essential insider tips, this book will have you crafting your own coffee creations in no time and there's even inspiration for flavored syrups and toppings for your full coffee experience. If you're looking to upgrade your coffee game, grab yourself a copy of this book and get started.